The Economic Impacts of
the Advanced Encryption
Standard, 1996–2017

Other titles in Annals of Science and Technology Policy

Nanotechnology: A Call for Policy Research
Joshua Gorsuch and Albert N. Link
ISBN: 978-1-68083-498-7

The Interweaving of Diffusion Research and American Science and Technology Policy
Irwin Feller
ISBN: 978-1-68083-474-1

In Search of Evidence-based Science Policy: From the Endless Frontier to SciSIP
Albert H. Teich
ISBN:978-1-68083-444-4

Measuring Science, Technology, and Innovation: A Review
Bronwyn H. Hall and Adam B. Jaffe
ISBN: 978-1-68083-400-0

The Economic Impacts of the Advanced Encryption Standard, 1996–2017

David P. Leech

Economic Analysis & Evaluation, LLC, VA 22314, USA
david.leech@starpower.net

Stacey Ferris

RM Advisory Services, LLC, VA 22314, USA
stacey.ferris@rmadvisory.com

John T. Scott

Dartmouth College, NH 03755, USA
john.t.scott@dartmouth.edu

Boston — Delft

Annals of Science and Technology Policy

Published, sold and distributed by:
now Publishers Inc.
PO Box 1024
Hanover, MA 02339
United States
Tel. +1-781-985-4510
www.nowpublishers.com
sales@nowpublishers.com

Outside North America:
now Publishers Inc.
PO Box 179
2600 AD Delft
The Netherlands
Tel. +31-6-51115274

The preferred citation for this publication is

David P. Leech and Stacey Ferris and John T. Scott. *The Economic Impacts of the Advanced Encryption Standard, 1996–2017.* Annals of Science and Technology Policy, vol. 3, no. 2, pp. 142–257, 2019.

ISBN: 978-1-68083-588-5
© 2019 David P. Leech and Stacey Ferris and John T. Scott

Annals of Science and Technology Policy
Volume 3, Issue 2, 2019
Editorial Board

Editorial Scope

Topics

Annals of Science and Technology Policy publishes survey and tutorial articles in the following topics:

- Literature reviews of technology and innovation policies

- Historical case studies of technology development and implementation

- Institutional histories of technology- and innovation-based organizations

- Analyses of policies attendant to technology development and adoption and diffusion

- Studies documenting the adoption and diffusion of technologies and subsequent consequences

- Studies of public and private research partnerships (cross sectional, over time, or case based)

- Assessments and evaluations of specific technology and innovation policies

- Analyses of ecosystems associated with the technology and/or innovation development

- Cross observational (e.g., cross-agency or cross-country) comparisons of technology and innovation policies

Information for Librarians

Annals of Science and Technology Policy, 2019, Volume 3, 4 issues. ISSN paper version 2475-1820. ISSN online version 2475-1812. Also available as a combined paper and online subscription.

Contents

The Economic Impacts of the Advanced Encryption Standard, 1996–2017

David P. Leech[1], Stacey Ferris[2] and John T. Scott[3]

[1] *Economic Analysis & Evaluation, LLC, VA 22314, USA;*
david.leech@starpower.net
[2] *RM Advisory Services, LLC, VA 22314, USA;*
stacey.ferris@rmadvisory.com
[3] *Dartmouth College, NH 03755, USA; john.t.scott@dartmouth.edu*

ABSTRACT

This paper evaluates the net social benefits of advanced encryption standards (AES), which is one of many areas where the National Institute for Standards and Technology (NIST) has promoted innovation and industrial competitiveness to ensure that public and private computer systems can protect the confidentiality, availability, and integrity of digital information in the face of ever more powerful computers and developments in the field of cryptography.

David P. Leech, Stacey Ferris and John T. Scott (2019), "The Economic Impacts of the Advanced Encryption Standard, 1996–2017", Annals of Science and Technology Policy: Vol. 3, No. 2, pp 142–257. DOI: 10.1561/110.00000010.

1

Introduction[1]

1.1 NIST's mission

One of the responsibilities of the federal government is "to provide for the general welfare" (U.S. Constitution). From an economic perspective this often entails the collaboration of industry associations and state and federal agencies to mitigate barriers to economic development that arise in the normal process of innovation. It is generally understood that creation and diffusion of new technology is the single most important contributor to the nation's long-term economic growth path.[2] There is also a consensus, among economists that study the innovation process, that reliance on market processes alone will result in underinvestment in research and development, from a social point of view.[3]

---

[1] This monograph is an extension of an earlier NIST report, *The Economic Impacts of the Advanced Encryption Standard, 1996–2017* (NIST GCR 18-017), September 2018.

[2] Albert Link and Donald Siegel, *Technological Change and Economic Performance*, Routledge, 2003.

[3] Stephen Martin and John T. Scott, "The Nature of Innovation Market Failure and the Design of Public Support for Private Iinnovation," *Research Policy*, Vol. 29, 2000, pp. 437–447.

Toward that goal of providing for the general economic welfare, the federal government invests over \$140 billion annually in R&D, a small part of which is allocated to the National Institute of Standard and Technology (NIST). These moneys are spent at NIST in an effort to fulfill its mission to "promote U.S. innovation and industrial competitiveness by advancing measurement science, standards, and technology in ways that enhance economic security and improve our quality of life."[4]

One of many areas in which NIST has promoted innovation and industrial competitiveness is in the area of advanced encryption standards to ensure that public and private computer systems can protect the confidentiality, availability, and integrity of digital information in the face of ever more powerful computers and developments in the field of cryptography. This monograph represents a step toward evaluating the net social benefits of advanced encryption standards.

Since its creation as the National Bureau of Standards (NBS) in 1901, NIST has partnered with industry to unleash American innovation and, consequently, worldwide innovation. Over the last couple of decades, NIST's understanding of the role of technology development and innovation in the process of economic growth, the role of standards in that growth process, and how to measure NIST's contributions to innovative progress have all improved significantly.[5]

NIST serves two overarching roles in the innovation process. One is an "honest broker" role. NIST brings its respected measurement technology and expertise to innumerable scientific and commercial interactions that revolve around how the performance of new products (from cholesterol molecules and DNA fragments to light emissions and nanotubes) and processes (from the time of day and computer clock time to how fires proceed and high-rise buildings collapse) is measured and how the innovations compare with existing products and their next-generation replacements. NIST's other overarching role is as a national

---

[4]https://www.nist.gov/director/pao/nist-general-information.

[5]See, for example, Gregory Tassey, "Making America Great Again," *Issues in Science and Technology*," Winter 2018, pp. 72–78; and "The Roles and Impacts of Technical Standards on Economic Growth and Implications for Innovation Policy," *Annals of Science and Technology Policy*, Vol. 1, No. 3, 2017; and Albert Link and John Scott, *The Theory and Practice of Public-Sector R&D Economic Impact Analysis*, Planning Report 11-1, NIST, January 2012.

channel of the highest international standards of measurement. Scientific research, technology development, innovation, and commercialization are global phenomena and international-scale interactions that determine the performance and conformance of traded goods and services and are more important than ever to economic security.

NIST routinely directs its vast technical expertise into technology partnering activities between NIST laboratories and industries, other Federal agencies, state and local Governments, the general public, and other nations. The goal of these efforts is to enable technology transfer to promote U.S. innovation and competitiveness. Toward that end, NIST has analyzed the economic impacts of scores of NIST-performed and NIST-managed programs. Cumulatively, these impact assessments are a rich source of lessons learned for NIST laboratory managers: describing why projects were developed, what partners were involved, what problems were addressed and how, and what difference the projects made both in terms of economic impacts and NIST's stewardship of U.S. tax dollars.

1.2 Economic impact assessment focus

The focus of this retrospective economic impact assessment is NIST's AES program, which began in 1996 and continues through today; however, for the purposes of economic measurement, this monograph bounds the assessment at 2017.

The AES program was initiated as its predecessor, the Data Encryption Standard (DES) Program, was winding down. In 2000, NIST first assessed the retrospective economic impact of the DES Program.[6] The program was assessed in the context of what is now referred to as the commercial "crypto revolution."[7]

Much has changed in the world of information technology and security since 2000. Contentious policy battles over trade in cryptographic products have been resolved; stronger cryptographic algorithms are in

---

[6]David Leech and Michael Chinworth, *The Economic Impacts of NIST's Data Encryption Standards Program*, Planning Report 01-2, U.S. Department of Commerce/NIST, September 2001.

[7]Steven Levy, *Crypto*, Viking, 2001, p. 164.

widespread use; information security concerns that were largely ignored by much of the public are now a significant focus of public attention; powerful wireless computers are toted in the pockets, briefcases, and shoulder bags of a broad swath of the worlds' adult population; and the technology and practices employed by nefarious information system hackers have risen to the status of tangible threats to national sovereignty.

The Trump Administration's Management Agenda calls on Federal agencies to improve the transfer of Federally-funded technologies from lab-to-market and the evaluation of its economic impact.[8] For NIST, intramural R&D is an important component of that Federal funding. This economic impact assessment is intended to revisit NIST's investments in the successor to the DES Program, understand the principal dimensions of its effects, and estimate the economic impact of NIST's AES program expenditures from its inception until today.

Within this monograph, Chapter 2 (Background) provides the ABCs of cryptography as it applies to the AES and an introduction to the computer networks that employ encryption systems. It further delves into the evolution of NIST's role as the Federal Government's authority on the computer security of civilian-focused agencies, the AES competition (1997–2000), and subsequent cryptographic validation programs including what these validation programs reveal about the composition of the encryption product market.

Chapter 3 (Economic Analysis Framework) characterizes how the AES program and subsequent dependent industry standards have functioned as economic policy tools that reduced the economic barriers of the 1990s to the development, commercialization, and application of cryptographic technologies, as well as their continuing indirect role in supporting the quality of encryption systems, reducing encryption system risks, and facilitating the growth of related industries. Chapter 3 also places the AES program in an industrial organizational context by describing the economic value chain of which the AES program is a part.

---

[8]https://www.whitehouse.gov/wp-content/uploads/2018/04/ThePresidentsManagementAgenda.pdf, p. 47.

Chapter 4 (Economic Assessment Impact Approach) discusses the selection of pre-survey interviews with subject matter experts, the design of the survey instrument, and survey execution.

Chapter 5 (Survey Results and Findings) describes survey results, compares selected qualitative survey findings to pre-survey expectations, describes the three-tiered approach to estimating economic impact in context of actual survey results, and reports the costs of NIST's AES program, 1996–2017.

Chapter 6 (Economic Impact of AES, 1996–2017) presents the results of the three-tiered approach to estimating the overall economic impacts of the AES program.

Chapter 7 (Overall Economic Impact Assessment Conclusions) provides a summary and conclusion of the analysis.

2

Background

2.1 Cryptography ABCs

Encryption is the process of converting plaintext into ciphertext using a
key. The ciphertext is only readable to key holders who can decrypt the
data. Decryption translates ciphertext back to plaintext. Cryptography
has become deeply interwoven in numerous facets of modern computer
operations. It is "used to perform or support several basic security
services: confidentiality, integrity authentication, source authentication,
authorization and non-repudiation."[1] Ancient Roman ciphers were
simple and limited to written alpha-numeric characters, but modern
cryptographic functions performed by computers can translate any data
that can be expressed in computer code, i.e., binary (1's and 0's), into
unreadable ciphertext. In simple terms, encryption and decryption is
the process of a computer conducting a highly complex math problem —
a problem so complex that it could not be done even using computer
speed, processing, and memory capacity without the key.

The two broadest categories of encryption systems are symmetric "secret-key" encryption and asymmetric "public-key" encryption.

---

[1]Elaine Barker, *Recommendation for Key Management, Part 1: General*, NIST
Special Publication 800-57 Part 1, Revision 4, 2016.

Symmetric secret-key encryption uses a single key known to both the sender and recipient for encryption and decryption. One of the greatest cryptography challenges in the 20th century was unravelling how to exchange secret keys when the sender and recipient are unable to physically meet. This puzzle was cracked in the 1970s by researchers at Stanford and the Massachusetts Institute of Technology (MIT, and the eventual founders of RSA Labs) and came to be known as public-key encryption.[2] Today, secret keys are typically encrypted using public-key encryption. Asymmetric public-key encryption makes two different keys: one public and one secret. The public key is openly available, so an authorized user can access this key to send an encrypted message to the private-key holder or verify the private-key holder's signature using their public key.

For a majority of Internet and network-based computer interactions, public-key encryption is used to establish a secure connection and verify computer/user identities, and secret-key encryption like AES is then used for bulk-data encryption. Symmetric secret-key cryptography can be further categorized as either stream ciphers or block ciphers, referring to whether data is encrypted one bit at a time or it is compiled into "blocks" of data that are encrypted in batches. AES is a symmetric block cipher.

Symmetric block ciphers organize plaintext data in blocks. The blocks can be visualized like the face of a Rubik's Cube with two bits of data in each square. Just as a Rubik's Cube with more blocks on each side is more difficult to solve, so a larger block in encryption increases the complexity of the mathematical functions. The block size of DES was 56 bits. AES more than doubles that and uses a block size of 128 bits.

The key is also arranged as a block and used to perform mathematical scrambling functions on the plaintext data to produce cipher text. The

---

[2]The history is recounted in detail in Steven Levy, *Crypto*, Viking, 2001. As explained therein, the private-sector researchers had independently rediscovered public-key cryptography that had actually been invented in the late 1960s and early 1970s by Government researchers within the British Communications Electronics Security Group (CESG) of the Government Communications Headquarters (GCHQ) — the British counterpart to the United States' National Security Agency (NSA), but the British intelligence agency had suppressed the discovery, keeping it a secret.

key itself is also subject to mathematical scrambling to create versions of
it. Use of multiple keys speeds up encryption and increases the security
when processing large amounts of data. The creators of AES described
it thusly: "A block cipher transforms *plaintext* blocks of a fixed length
n_b to *ciphertext* blocks of the same length under the influence of a cipher
key k."[3]

Figure 2.1 provides a general understanding of how AES functions.[4]
Each round performs mathematical scrambling using the key, which
is a set of randomly generated alphanumeric characters organized like
the data. The number of rounds performed depends on the key size,
as shown in the box to the right where "R" stands for "rounds". For a
128-bit key, 10 rounds of scrambling are performed; for a 192-bit key,
12 rounds of scrambling; and for a 256-bit key, 14 rounds of encryption
scrambling occur.

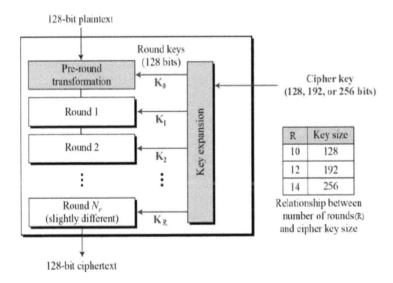

Figure 2.1: How the AES algorithm works.

---

[3]Vincent Rijmen and Joan Daemen, *The Design of Rijndael, AES — The
Advanced Encryption Standard.* Springer-Verlag publishing, 2002, p. 23.

[4]http://www.tutorialspoint.com/cryptography/advanced_encryption_
standard.htm.

Cryptographic strength increases with longer keys and larger block sizes. The key is a string of alpha-numeric characters. Designed in the early 1970s, DES had 56-bit keys, which translated to roughly 72 quadrillion (72,000,000,000,000,000) possible keys. AES has key size options of 128, 194, and 256, providing for various levels of security. For most applications, 128-bit keys are employed. During the period covered by this analysis (1996–2017), the U.S. National Security Agency (NSA) approved AES-256 as acceptable for protecting up to top-secret classified data; by comparison, DES was approved for protecting unclassified, sensitive data. The smallest 128-bit key size of AES has 2,128 possible keys, or approximately:

340,000,000,000,000,000,000,000,000,000,000,000,000 possible keys.[5]

Brute force cracking AES is widely considered unfeasible due to the immense time and computer processing resources needed to cycle through possible keys. To date, AES has not been successfully attacked in this manner and it is generally held by NIST and the cryptographic community that even quantum computers will not, in the near term, be able to brute force crack data secured by AES-256.[6]

At a high level, breaking a cipher can be done one of two ways: either run through key options until the correct key is found (brute force attacks), or perform cryptanalysis, that is, pattern and probability analysis to guess plaintext–ciphertext pairs and decrypt from there. Block ciphers arrange data in blocks for encryption. Longer chains of data with thousands of blocks hold an increased risk of having two identical blocks, which increases the susceptibility to cryptanalysis. DES became susceptible to both types of attacks. The AES developers noted that, "resistance against these two attacks is the most important criterion in the design of Rijndael."[7] Various modes of operation available

---

[5] This number is pronounced "three hundred forty undecillions." http://www.webmath.com/_answer.php

[6] Lily Chen *et al.*, *Report on Post-Quantum Cryptography* (NISTIR 8105 DRAFT), February 2016, p. 3. (Re., symmetric key systems, "We don't know that Grover's algorithm will ever be practically relevant, but if it is, doubling the key size will be sufficient to preserve security.")

[7] Rijmen and Daemen, op. cit., p. 81.; Rijndael is the name of the cipher chosen for the AES.

with AES address this potential weakness by performing additional block setup steps to reduce the probability of inadvertent duplications or other weaknesses.

AES can operate in five different confidentiality modes: Electronic Codebook (ECB), Cipher Block Chaining (CBC), Cipher Feedback (CFB), Output Feedback (OFB), and Counter (CTR) modes.[8] The mode used will depend upon the specific implementation of encryption and how keys are generated, stored, and validated. The AES modes of operation were implemented with an eye towards covering any potential weak points that would create analyzable information. The modes of operation available in an encryption hardware or software unit are determined when the AES code is implemented. Multiple modes can be available for use in one module, and they are selected based on the nature of the data that will be encrypted and decrypted.

Modes of operation can be thought of metaphorically: A person dresses according to the anticipated weather. If it is going to be sunny and warm, the person will not wear a jacket. If it will be windy and rainy, they will wear a jacket and bring an umbrella. The person is like AES and does not change, but what the person is wrapped or dressed in — that is, the person's "mode of operation" — does change according to the anticipated weather, or for AES, its modes of operation are set based on the anticipated data it will encounter.

2.2   Elements of an encryption system

An "encryption system" is defined here to be information systems that use hardware and software modules to perform core encryption processing, key generation, key management, and any other secure data storage and transmission. Encryption system engineers denote two types of data that can be secured via encryption:

1. **Data at rest**, or stored data: data resident on a device (e.g., a hard drive or smartphone) that are neither being manipulated nor otherwise processed.

---

[8]https://csrc.nist.gov/Projects/Block-Cipher-Techniques/BCM/Current-Modes.

2. **Data in motion**, or data in transit: data being sent between various points.[9]

Data is held, processed, and transmitted by a variety of hardware and software modules. *Encryption hardware* includes storage devices, network appliances, standalone encryption engines and accelerators, access and authentication systems, radios, and telephones. *Encryption software* includes cryptographic libraries, developers' toolkits, dedicated software encryption processors or accelerators, dedicated software key management, authentication system interfaces, virtual network routers, switches, and firewalls, and virtual network management software.

Figure 2.2 depicts a typical encryption system for cloud hosting, data centers, and other large data processing/holding operations. Within this figure, the end user terminal sends requests or data to remote servers. The remote servers handle thousands of requests per minute, so they offload key generation and some encryption work to dedicated encryption units to achieve processing efficiencies.

Figure 2.3 illustrates the use of encryption for access controls in a smaller encryption system. In this small-scale encryption system, all

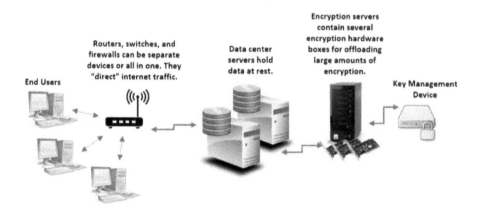

Figure 2.2: Large encryption system.

---

[9]Chris Jaikaran, *Encryption: Frequently Asked Questions*, Congressional Research Service, September 28, 2016.

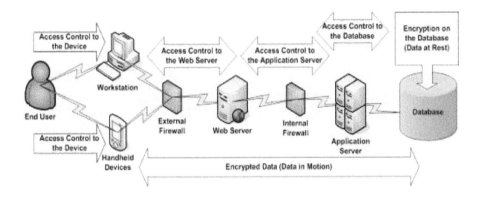

Figure 2.3: Small encryption system.[10]

encryption processing is performed within the devices and no work is offloaded. As an encryption system gets smaller, it will compress and shrink encryption processes into as few discrete hardware and software modules as possible to increase speed and efficiency. Figure 2.3 depicts the end user as using either a computer or handheld device; however, the array of devices captured by the phrase "Internet of Things" has the potential to extend an encryption system beyond the end-user terminal and network infrastructure to include such items as home appliances, vehicles, wearable technology, bridges, railway tracks, onshore and offshore wind-farms, and the like.

2.3 The U.S. encryption regulatory environment

Federal Information Processing Standards, or FIPS, were born in the Brooks Act of 1965 and evolved with the changing roles of the Department of Commerce and NIST over time. Congressman Jack Brooks, the chairman of the Government Activities Subcommittee of the Committee on Government Operations of the House, introduced the Brooks Bill (H.R. 4845) in 1965 to amend Title I of the Federal Property and Administration Services Act of 1949 to correct known deficiencies in government automated data processing management, one

---

[10]Source: https://www.cdc.gov/cancer/npcr/tools/security/encryption2.htm.

of which was a lack of standardization and compatibility. What came to be known as "the Brooks Act" (Public Law 89-306, 1965) is regarded as the earliest significant congressional action affecting Federal use of information technology.[11] It assigned authority to the Department of Commerce to make recommendations for uniform Federal automatic data processing standards.[12] Implementation of the act called for a new publication series of automatic data processing standards, to be called Federal Information Processing Standards Publications, "FIPS PUBS."[13]

FIPS have arguably grown in stature and importance over time, particularly as computer-based technology finds its way into every aspect of both public and private sector operations. NIST's role as an honest broker in developing FIPS has brought both domestic and international industry and academia to the table.

NIST first tackled symmetric block encryption with FIPS-46, the Data Encryption Standard (DES), published in 1977. DES dominated the 1980s when encryption was still primarily considered a national security and defense concern. In a 1988 survey, the Government Accountability Office (GAO) reported 97% of all reported sensitive systems, or approximately 52,000 sensitive Government systems, were within the Department of Defense (DoD). It comes as no surprise then that the NSA, the intelligence agency founded to create and unravel WWII encrypted communications, was heavily involved in encryption algorithms design and use in the Federal space.

From the 1950s through the 1990s, the NSA was the dominant voice in Federal cryptographic regulation matters. The agency advocated for the export limits of encryption to be set at 40-bit keys, under the

---

[11]U.S. Congress, Office of Technology Assessment, Federal Government Information Technology: Management, Security, and Congressional Oversight, OTA-CIT-297 (Washington, D.C.: U.S. Government Printing Office, February 1986).

[12]Charles I. Willis, *The Brooks Act, Is It Relevant Today?* (Masters Thesis) Naval Postgraduate School, June 1994, pp. 8–13; Public Law 89-306, October 30, 1965. *An act to provide for the economic and efficient purchase, lease, maintenance, operation, and utilization of automatic data processing equipment by Federal departments and agencies.*

[13]Elio Passaglia, *A Unique Institution: The National Bureau of Standards 1950– 1969*, U.S. Government Printing Office, 1999, pp. 558–560.

conviction that encryption was a matter of national security. Indeed, the primary users of encryption for much of the 20th century were national security-related entities. Even DES with its 56-bit keys was considered too strong for export, and thus IBM (the DES creator) also developed a weaker 40-bit key version for use in exported hardware and software.[14] The NSA had worked closely with IBM on the development of DES, and reportedly made some unexplained changes to the nature of the S-boxes used in the block cipher.[15] As a consequence, the reputation of DES suffered in the eyes of many commercial players due to the shrouded involvement of the NSA in its development.

In the DES era, responsibility for computer security was spread among a number of agencies including the DoD, NSA, General Services Administration (GSA), and the National Bureau of Standards (NBS, later NIST). A report by the House of Representatives, Committee on Science, Space, and Technology, accompanying the Computer Security Act (CSA) of 1987, worried that a "lack of coordination" weakened U.S. computer security policy:

> This mixture of laws, regulations, and responsible agencies has raised concern that Federal computer security policy is lacking direction and forcefulness in some areas, yet has created overlapping and duplication of effort in other areas.[16]

The CSA of 1987 attempted to redress this situation by moving responsibility for computer security to the agency level and consolidating more authority under the Department of Commerce. It required Federal agencies to identify systems with sensitive information and provide training on security measures to employees. However, it provided limited direction on how to define a sensitive system and what

---

[14] https://en.wikipedia.org/wiki/Data_Encryption_Standard#cite_note-6.

[15] In the description of how encryption works, the S-boxes were likened to the faces of a Rubik's Cube. Encryption setup involves organizing data into these boxes. The NSA's involvement and sometimes specific insistence on certain design elements fueled private sector fears that there was an intentional Government "backdoor" in the DES algorithm. General sentiment suggests that NIST successfully avoided this with AES by hosting a public and global AES competition.

[16] https://csrc.nist.gov/csrc/media/projects/ispab/documents/csa_87.txt.

constituted sufficient training and security measures. A 1988 GAO audit of Federal compliance with the CSA indicated unequal and uncoordinated efforts across agencies as they developed their own internal criteria for identifying sensitive systems and providing training and security.[17]

The 1990s heralded the introduction of the World Wide Web to the greater public, and excitement around this new technology fueled rapid economic expansion in computer technology. Certainly, by the time the 21st century dawned, there was tremendous national excitement and energy around computer technologies. Federal agencies and the technology companies that served them were anticipating the new AES. The controversy over export policy continued to rage even as the AES project was launched in 1996. The controversy was not resolved, so far as the export market was concerned, until 2000 when the newly in-charge Department of Commerce, Bureau of Export Administration, significantly relaxed restrictions on cryptographic hardware and software products by "multilaterally decontrol[ling] mass market encryption commodities and software up to and including 64-bits... making them eligible for export and re-export to all destinations."[18] As commercial mass-market products using AES began rolling out in the following years, they were eligible for export. The AES source code was made freely available worldwide, and over time has become a trusted algorithm across the globe.[19]

In July 2001, the e-Government Act was introduced to Congress, which evolved into the 2002 Federal Information Security Management Act (FISMA). FISMA recognized that the Government needed a stronger framework for operating within the emerging Internet and digital technology spaces. Most significantly, FISMA prohibited agencies from waiving compliance with computer security measures, which was

---

[17]U.S. General Accounting Office, *Computer Security: Status of Compliance with the Computer Security Act of 1987*, September 1988. GAO/IMTEC-88-61BR. https://www.gao.gov/assets/80/77177.pdf.

[18]https://epic.org/crypto/export_controls/finalregs.pdf. Rule amendments for the Bureau of Export Administration, January 10, 2000. RIN 0694-AC11.

[19]AES is included in European and Japanese Government recommended encryption algorithm lists, among others.

permitted under previous legislation. FISMA also required NIST to do the following:

- Establish standards for categorizing information and information systems according to ranges of risk levels (See FIPS-199 and -200);

- Develop minimum security requirements for information and information systems in each of the risk categories;

- Develop guidelines for detection and handling of information security incidents; and

- Develop guidelines, in conjunction with the DoD, for identifying an information system as a national security system.[20]

In 2004, the GAO issued guidance for FISMA compliance that highlighted cryptography as an "integral part of an effectively enforced information security policy."[21]

Beyond the Federal Government, laws and regulations passed between 1996 and 2004 specifically called for the use of encryption in the financial, healthcare, and retail industries, as well as in all publicly traded companies. The most significant of these laws and regulations are highlighted in Figure 2.4. In turn, these industries and companies looked to established industry standards for guidance. Industry standards bodies often reference FIPS and use them as a foundation for industry-specific standards; however, the only entities required by Federal law to use certified FIPS ciphers are Federal Government agencies.

As a result of increased legislation, relaxed encryption export regulation, and the sheer volume of buying power that the Federal Government possesses, FIPS standards have influenced nearly every sector of the U.S. economy in some way.

---

[20] *Federal Information Security* (GAO 17-549), United States Government Accountability Office, September 2017.

[21] *Information Security: Technologies to Secure Federal Systems*, GAO-04-467, March 2004.

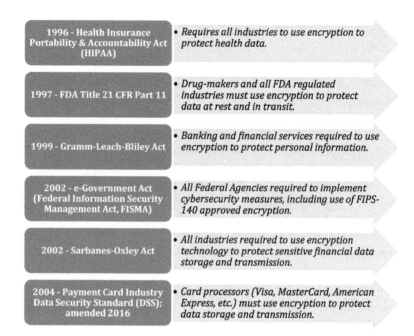

Figure 2.4: Laws and regulations requiring use of encryption by the private sector.

2.4 The genesis of AES

2.4.1 Prelude to AES: It was not always thus

In historical context, the AES competition was a remarkable event as it followed two decades of acrimony between the commercial sector's efforts to cash in on the developments of private sector cryptographic innovation, and the efforts of largely secret government agencies trying to gain control of cryptography as their sole province in the post-WWII era. Those agencies were initially exposed to the wider public — and many budding civilian cryptographers — by academic and other independent critics, for example, in workshops organized by NIST in the 1970s to review the draft of FIPS-46.[22]

NIST straddled that divide for a long time, beginning with Brooks Act of 1965. As early as 1993, NIST noted that DES was increasingly

---

[22]Levy, op. cit., pp. 56–65.

not up to par for the demands put upon it by computer technology utilized at the time. It was evident that if computer power continued to increase at a steady pace, DES would be outdated and unusable by the end of the decade. Indeed, by the end of the 1990s, cryptanalysts had demonstrated that DES could be hacked in less than 24 hours.[23] In 1993, NIST reviewed and reaffirmed DES for another five years (FIPS-46-2), but with a warning that it would not be reaffirmed in 1998. In 1999 Federal agencies and their suppliers and contractors were advised to begin implementing Triple DES (TDES) until an advanced encryption algorithm was developed.[24]

In essence, TDES simply runs DES three times in a row using two or three unique keys. However, if a gate is ineffective, putting up two more gates does not stop intruders, it merely delays them. Similarly, TDES delays all encryption processes, including encrypting and decrypting activities. Nonetheless, TDES remains in use today, and in fact, 3-Key TDES is approved by NIST through approximately 2030.[25]

In the mid-1990s, the Clinger-Cohen Act noted that FIPS standards were often duplicative of existing industry standards. NIST declared, "We will issue FIPS only where there are compelling Federal Government requirements."[26] Considering that there were already several block cipher alternatives to DES at the time — such as Blowfish, IDEA, and RC5 — why would NIST open a competition to create a new algorithm and FIPS? Individuals working in the mid-1990s commented that the atmosphere was one of confusion and lack of interoperability. None of the alternatives had been able to establish itself as a significantly better option than DES or TDES. As such, NIST determined that a sufficient

---

[23]In 1997, an RSA Labs cryptanalysis challenge team successfully brute force attacked DES after running through 25% of the 72 quadrillion keys or about 18 quadrillion keys. In 1999, another cryptanalysis team used a network of almost 100,000 PCs connected through the Internet to crack DES in 22 hours and 15 minutes. http://www.tjscott.net/crypto/des.hack.htm.

[24]Miles Smid, "Developing the Advanced Encryption Standard," mimeo, February 2, 2018, p. 4.

[25]Barker, 2016, op. cit., pp. 55–56.

[26]*Information Technology Laboratory Technical Accomplishments 1996* (NISTIR 5938), U.S. Department of Commerce, January 1997, pg. 7.

industry standard for symmetric block encryption did not exist, and
that NIST leadership, in the form of a new FIPS, was required.[27]

2.4.2   Competition and criteria

Anticipating the need for high-quality cryptography, in 1996 the Computer Security Division (CSD) of NIST's Information Technology Laboratory (ITL) initiated planning the development of new advanced
cryptographic algorithm standards for encryption, digital signatures, and
key exchange.[28] In the September 1997 Federal Register, NIST solicited
submissions for the Advanced Encryption Algorithm, which would
be "an unclassified, publicly disclosed encryption algorithm available
royalty-free worldwide that is capable of protecting sensitive Government
information well into the next century."[29] The solicitation set out three
minimum acceptability requirements for candidates to be considered
"complete and proper":

1. The algorithm must implement symmetric (secret) key cryptography.

2. The algorithm must be a block cipher.

3. The candidate algorithm shall be capable of supporting key-block
   combinations with sizes of 128–128, 192–128, and 256–128 bits.

Submissions would be evaluated on overall security, speed, and
implementation characteristics across a variety of hardware and software.
Further, the announcement specified that the competition would involve
public comment rounds to openly critique candidates as well as unearth
any potential intellectual property or other conflicts. The winning
algorithm would be made publicly available and royalty free upon
selection.

---

[27] Smid, op. cit.

[28] U.S. Department of Commerce, January 1997, op. cit., p. 14.

[29] *Federal Register*, September 12, 1997, "Announcing Request for Candidate
Algorithm Nominations for the Advanced Encryption Standard, A Notice by the
National Institutes of Standards and Technology," Document Citation: 62 FR 48051.
Document Number: 97-24214.

Table 2.1: AES competition candidate algorithms.

Algorithm	Submitter(s)	Submitter type	Country(ies)
		Finalists	
Rijndael	**Daemen and Rijmen**	**Researchers**	**Belgium**
Serpent	Anderson, Biham, Knudsen	Researchers	UK, Israel, Denmark
Mars	IBM	Company	USA
RC6	RSA	Company	USA
Twofish	Counterpane	Company	USA
		Other Candidate Algorithms	
CAST-256	Entrust	Company	Canada
Crypton	Future Systems	Company	South Korea
DEAL	Outerbridge, Knudsen	Researchers	USA, Denmark
DFC	ENS-CNRS	Researchers	France
E2	NTT	Company	Japan
Frog	TecApro	Company	Costa Rica
HPC	Schroeppel	Researcher	USA
LOKI97	Brown *et al.*	Researchers	Australia
Magenta	Deutsche Telekom	Company	Germany
SAFER+	Cylink	Company	USA

Candidate algorithms poured in from around the globe: the United States, Europe, Asia, and Latin America all had submissions. In total, NIST received 21 submissions that were presented at a public conference in 1998. During the conference, the submissions were openly challenged and evaluated, and six were eliminated. Fifteen submissions, shown in Table 2.1, were deemed to meet the minimum acceptability requirements. NIST's James Foti said of the decision to open the competition to international submissions, "We worked really hard to consider the public perception of what we were doing."[30]

Qualified submissions were further evaluated on three factors: security, cost, and implementation flexibility. The security factor was deemed the most important, covering "resistance of the algorithm to cryptanalysis, soundness of its mathematical basis, randomness of the algorithm output, and relative security as compared to other candidates." The cost factor included "licensing requirements, computational efficiency

---

[30]https://gcn.com/Articles/2001/06/28/NIST-goes-public-to-keep-Federal-secrets.aspx.

(speed) on various platforms, and memory requirements" — all aspects more important to hardware implementations than software. Finally, the algorithm needed to display certain characteristics including "flexibility, hardware and software suitability, and algorithm simplicity."[31]

The candidate algorithms were analyzed on ANSI C and JAVA™ implementations. The ANSI C implementations "focused on speed... on various desktop systems, using different combinations of processors, operating systems, and compilers." The JAVA™ implementations were tested for "speed and memory usage on a desktop system".[32]

2.4.3 Down-select and worldwide cryptanalysis

NIST encouraged participation from industry, academia, and government experts both as submitters and in public comment rounds. NIST's ITL hosted two public conferences, the first in Ventura, CA in 1998 and the second in Rome, Italy in 1999, to encourage open participation in the evaluation process. The first conference allowed the 15 accepted submitters to "formally present their candidate algorithms and design philosophy" as well as allow for open discourse and analysis of the submissions. NIST established "electronic discussion pages for each candidate" to allow for discussion of the algorithms prior to any submission of formal comments or feedback to NIST.[33]

During NIST's evaluation of the five AES finalists, Rijndael emerged as distinctly fast and efficient with "a low ROM requirement and very low RAM requirement. Both encryption and decryption are at least twice as fast as any other finalist."[34] While it ranked lower on inherent security than other competitors, it was simpler and more cost effective to implement across a range of software and hardware. Rijndael's simple structure relied only on "Boolean operations, table

---

[31] James Nechvatal *et al.*, *Report on the Development of the Advanced Encryption Standard (AES)*, Computer Security Division, Information Technology Laboratory, NIST, October 2, 2000, pp. 9–11.

[32] Ibid., p. 11.

[33] Edward Roback and Morris Dworkin, "Conference Report" (First Advanced Encryption Standard (AES) Candidate Conference, Ventura, CA, August 20–22, 1998), *Journal of Research of the National Institute of Standards and Technology*, Vol. 104, No. 1, January–February 1999.

[34] Nechvatal *et al.*, 2000, op. cit., p. 40.

lookups, and fixed shifts/rotations," which were determined to be "the easiest to defend against attacks."[35] At the time, NIST observed that Rijndael's speed decreased on 192-bit and 256-bit tests; however, significant improvements in computing power have since made AES-256 a feasible option for a wide range of devices and implementations.

As part of the evaluation, NIST solicited comments from "industry, academia, standards bodies, and the public" in order to "narrow the field of candidate algorithms to five or fewer."[36] Based on the comments and feedback, five finalists, shown in Table 2.1, were chosen and subjected to more intensive testing and scrutiny, as well as a second round of public comments from August 1999 through May 2000.

2.4.4 Final selection

In October 2000, NIST published a whitepaper detailing the five finalists and the results of the competition evaluations. The paper nominated Rijndael to become the Advanced Encryption Algorithm and detailed the results of analysis in the three primary categories: strength, speed, and implementation flexibility.

Strength

The strength of an encryption algorithm is described in terms of its security margin. The security margin "indicates the resistance of the cipher against improvements of known types of cryptanalysis."[37] MARS, Serpent, and Twofish all received security ratings of "high," while RC6 and Rijndael received "adequate" security margin ratings. The evaluators found Rijndael difficult to evaluate because it had three different key sizes: 128, 192, and 256. Some expressed concern that Rijndael's relatively simple structure created cryptanalysis vulnerability; however, the same simplicity also made Rijndael "the easiest to defend against attacks" as well as making it significantly faster than the other candidates.[38]

---

[35] Ibid., p. 66.
[36] *1998 ITL Technical Accomplishments* (NISTIR 6254), NIST, October 1998, p. 14.
[37] Rijmen and Daemen, op. cit., p. 63.
[38] Nechvatal *et al.*, op. cit., p. 66.

Speed

One of the major factors in evaluating a cipher's speed is the rate at which it can calculate and apply a key schedule. When encrypting large amounts of data, multiple variations in the original key are used. These variations are contained in a key schedule, which is determined at the point encryption is initiated. Key schedule setup and key generation are therefore core components of cipher operation. For encryption, decryption, and key setup, the evaluators described MARS as an average performer, Serpent was low-end performance, Twofish varied across platforms but had low-end key setup, RC6 had average to high-end performance, and Rijndael consistently had high-end performance.

Implementation flexibility

Implementation configurations matter since "doubling the size of an encryption program may make little difference on a general-purpose computer with a large memory, but doubling the area used in a hardware device typically more than doubles the cost of the device."[39] Selecting an algorithm with low memory requirements was preferable. Broadly, MARS, RC6, and Serpent were deemed too slow and demanding on random access memory. Twofish was faster than these but had a high memory requirement. Rijndael had the lowest memory requirement and ran significantly faster than the other candidates.

The following year of 2001 entailed NIST developing detailed implementation guidance and operational modes (AES has five modes which vary depending on the implementation environment). In early 2001, NIST released a draft FIPS-197 for comments. The official FIPS-197 formally selecting Rijndael as the AES was published in December 2001. Some thought that the AES should include multiple algorithms, and NIST briefly considered including both Rijndael and Serpent; however, the decision to only have one algorithm with different key sizes was to "decrease the complexity of implementations" and to have the effect of "lowering costs and promoting interoperability."[40]

---

[39]Nechvatal *et al.*, op. cit., p. 41.

[40]Faranak Nekoogar, "Digital Cryptography: Rijndael Encryption and AES Applications," October 11, 2001. https://www.eetimes.com/document.asp?doc_id=1275908, accessed September 10, 2017.

NIST's October 2000 report on the five competitor algorithms described the significant challenge of predicting future technology and selecting an algorithm that would serve well for decades. Since they desired an algorithm that could last several decades, adaptability to and flexibility for a variety of platforms was paramount. In the 16 years since the release of AES, computer technology has expanded rapidly across platforms, applications, and hardware, from smart phones and virtual reality to cloud computing, self-driving cars, and big data analysis. A single laptop can hold the computing power of a mainframe computer center of earlier decades. In recent years, the economy has witnessed explosive growth of e-commerce, cryptocurrency mining and markets, online gaming and social networks, and quantum computing, which is now in its infancy and anticipated to come to market around 2030.

According to Kevin Curran, a senior member of the Institute of Electrical and Electronics Engineers (IEEE) and a professor of cybersecurity at Ulster University:

> When quantum computing becomes a reality, many public-key algorithms will be obsolete... However, encryption schemes like AES, with large keys, will be safe from quantum computers for the time being. ... To break current cryptosystems, quantum computers must have between 500 and 2,000 qubits... However, existing quantum computers that we know about only operate with less than 15 qubits at present, so there is no immediate worry.[41]

Thus far, Rijndael is living up to its promise as an adaptable and strong encryption algorithm.

The value of the NIST work was recognized by both Government and industry. In 2001, the AES team received the Department of Commerce's Gold Medal Award for Leadership and the RSA Public Policy Award for significant contributions to the application of cryptographic technologies

---

[41] http://www.technewsworld.com/story/84837.html, accessed September 27, 2017.

towards the advancement of personal privacy, civil justice, and basic human rights.[42]

2.4.5   Cryptographic algorithm/module validation program

NIST's work did not end in 2001. New computer technology and advancements require constant evaluation of AES modes and implementations. To provide assurance concerning AES and other cryptographic implementations, NIST sponsors the Cryptographic Algorithm Validation Program (CAVP) and Cryptographic Module Validation Program (CMVP). These programs are the interface between NIST's approved algorithms and the industries that implement them in products and services. The testing is done through pre-approved labs using NIST methodology, and passing implementations receive an FIPS-140 validation certificate which is published on the NIST CSD website.

FIPS-140-2 lays out the minimum requirements for cryptography considered suitable for Federal Government use. Federal agencies are required to use validated cryptographic modules and/or products containing validated modules, referred to as "being FIPS-140 compliant." NIST is clear that use of non-validated cryptography is viewed as "providing no protection to the information or data."[43] NIST established the programs in 1995 to provide testing and validation services for cryptographic implementations and modules to IT hardware and software manufacturers, integrators, and developers. Once validated, a module is eligible for use by Federal agencies.

The Cryptographic Algorithm Validation Program (CAVP) tests the encryption algorithms coding and mode of operation parameters. This test is brief and primarily involves encrypting and decrypting sets of data to ensure the submitted code functions as intended. The Cryptographic Module Validation Program (CMVP) is a more rigorous set of tests that provide validation concerning the hardware or software module that contains cryptography. The CMVP requirements cover

---

[42] *Information Technology Laboratory Technical Accomplishments 2001* (NISTIR 6815), NIST, November, 2001, p. 42.

[43] https://csrc.nist.gov/Projects/Cryptographic-Module-Validation-Program, heading "Use of Unvalidated Cryptographic Modules by Federal Agencies and Departments."

design and implementation of the cryptographic algorithm, the physical environment and security, operational modes and environment, key management, electromagnetic compatibility, and ability to withstand attacks, among other things. "Module" is a broad term covering a wide variety of products. Modules range from a standalone hardware black box that sits between a computer's hard drive and external access and encrypts data that passes through it to a software library file built into an operating system that provides encryption instructions and code for other programs to reference and use in their operations.

Cryptographic and Security Testing (CST) laboratories are authorized by NIST, through the National Voluntary Laboratory Accreditation Program (NVLAP), to perform CAVP and CMVP testing. There are currently 21 CST labs, located internationally.[44] The CST laboratories perform CAVP and CMVP testing with validation tools developed by NIST and provided to the laboratories.

In the 16 years from January 2002 through December 2017, there have been 2,521 CMVP certificates issued for modules with AES implementations. Of these, 1,034 are active certificates and 1,487 are historical or revoked certificates. No duplication exists between historical and active certificates in the CMVP database.[45] A certificate for a distinct module generally includes multiple encryption algorithms, meaning it can use all the listed algorithms or is interoperable with other systems that use them.

With the assistance of a few CST lab directors, certified modules listed on NIST's website were classified by major product type. Table 2.2 ranks all historical and active module certificates containing AES by major product type.

Based on a careful reading of each certificate including AES, modules can be further classified into the hardware and software product subtypes, as described in Table 2.3.[46]

---

[44]https://www-s.nist.gov/niws/index.cfm?event=directory.results.

[45]https://csrc.nist.gov/Projects/Cryptographic-Module-Validation-Program.

[46]"Firmware," while a valid category, makes up less than 1% of CMVP certifications, and is therefore not included in this table.

Table 2.2: AES CMVP certificates by major product type.

Module type	Percent of total AES certifications (%)	Number of certifications
Network appliance	34.8	878
Processor	30.1	760
Crypto library	11.1	279
Storage	7.6	192
Authentication system	4.8	122
Radio	3.5	88
Toolkit	3.3	82
Key management	3.2	80
Digital cinema projector	1.6	40

Table 2.3: CMVP module product types and subtypes.

Module type	Hardware subtype	Software subtype
Storage	Solid state, hard drives, tape drives, USB drives, and in-line storage encryption devices	N/A
Network device	Routers, switches, mobility controllers, firewalls, network management devices	Virtual routers, virtual switches, virtual firewalls, virtual network management software
Cryptographic library	N/A	Cryptographic libraries
Toolkits	N/A	Cryptographic toolkits contain software developer tools to assist in implementing encryption capability
Encryption engines	Standalone encryption processor device (hardware security module) — frequently includes key management functions	Software-based encryption processors use existing hardware CPU to perform encryption, and generally include key management functions

(Continued)

Table 2.3: (*Continued*)

Module type	Hardware subtype	Software subtype
Key management	Standalone key management device for generating, storing, and securely destroying keys	Software-based Key management program
Accelerators	Standalone encryption accelerator device — used to offload encryption in data centers and heavy traffic networks	Software-based encryption acceleration program
Authentication system	Hardware components include ID cards, chips, and chip readers	Software modules include smart card applications, encryption processor programs, card/chip reader program
Other or specialty devices	Other hardware devices: radios, digital cinema projectors, postal meters, printers and telephones	Other encryption software: radios

3

Economic Analysis Framework

3.1 FIPS in economic context

This section provides a brief introduction to the economic significance of FIPS: the switching costs that a new FIPS entails; FIPS as public goods; as market-failure mitigating tools; and as infra-technology. The discussion provides some context for understanding the purpose of survey questions posed to respondents, the survey results, and the economic impact calculations.

3.1.1 Encryption systems and switching costs

An information *system* enables information to be stored, searched, retrieved, copied, filtered, manipulated, transmitted, received, and secured. Information systems typically consist of multiple pieces of hardware and software that require specialized training and that must be integrated to function effectively.[1] The "networked" nature of the information system has implications for its value to users: the value of

---

[1] Gregory Tassey "The Roles and Impacts of Technical Standards on Economic Growth and Implications for Innovation Policy," *Annals of Science and Technology Policy*, Vol. 1, No. 3, 2017, p. 223.

connecting depends on the number of other users already connected to it.[2] This is true of railroad networks, ATM networks, email networks, and even fire hydrant networks — an example that will be taken up in Section 3.1.5.

An industry rule of thumb, referred to as "Metcalf's Law," holds that if there are n people in a network, the value of the network to each of them is proportional to the number of other users, and the total value of the network (to all the users) is proportional to $n \times (n-1)$ or $n^2 - n$. Accordingly, if the value of the network to a single user is \$1 for each other user on the network, then a network of size 10 has a total value of approximately \$100, and if the size of the network is 100, the approximate total value is \$10,000, a 100-fold increase in the network's value to all users for only a 10-fold increase in network size.[3]

New technologies that are incompatible with popular networks, or users considering a change of networks, must overcome the costs of switching from one implementation of a technology to another, i.e., "switching costs." That can be a high hurdle. Switching costs include all the costs required to move from one system to another. In the case of encryption, switching costs might include the cost of new hardware, new software, additional staff, or additional training. For providers of the new incompatible network technology, for example an encryption system based on AES rather than DES or TDES, it means overcoming the combined switching costs to users of the rival network, a factor working to the distinct advantage of incumbents.[4] In other words, collective switching costs encourage *lock-in* from both the users' and the providers' perspectives, a phenomenon also known as the "installed base effect."[5] Lock-in tends to be durable because specialized databases — the information that information systems store, search, retrieve, copy, filter, manipulate, transmit, receive, and secure — grow over time and thereby, all else remaining equal, increase the costs of transitioning to alternative networks.[6] Of course, lock-in can be overcome by new service

---

[2]Shapiro and Varian, op. cit., p. 174.
[3]Ibid., p. 184.
[4]Ibid., p. 184.
[5]Ibid., pp. 133–134.
[6]Ibid., pp. 122–123.

providers, but it relies on delivering value in excess of total switching costs.[7]

In relation to encryption, different algorithms require different hardware and software implementations to operate effectively. DES and TDES were the most commonly used symmetric block algorithms prior to AES.[8] Switching costs to move from DES/TDES to AES could include the costs of new hardware, new software, software updates, new training, and migrating stored data to the new algorithm (decrypting and re-encrypting stored data). Appendix A contains a historical case study of encryption system switching costs involved in the transition from DES to TDES to AES in the banking and finance sector.

3.1.2 Interoperability, compatibility, and standardization

Two communication networks lack interoperability if subscribers on one network cannot communicate with those on the other network. Two hardware/software systems are incompatible if the components of one system do not work with components of the other system.[9] Encryption system costs rise when more than one encryption "language," or algorithm, is used to communicate with all the computers in the network: longer processing time requires more power; transmitting data may be slower; maintenance and repair may be more complex. As more computers use the same language, costs decrease and ease of use increases.

Standardization expands the benefits of networks by enhancing interoperability and compatibility, making it possible for one network to share information with a larger network, thereby attracting more consumers. Standards play a large role where information technology is ascendant. Shapiro and Varian claim that formal standard-setting processes have never been more important to market competition.[10] In addition to enhancing network externalities, standards tend to reduce risk to consumers by bolstering the credibility of technology, reducing

---

[7]Ibid., pp. 111–115.

[8]This statement is specifically about symmetric block ciphers.

[9]http://www.testingstandards.co.uk/interop_et_al.htm.

[10]Shapiro and Varian, op. cit., p. 237.

consumer lock-in if standards are open, shifting the locus of competition from competing for market dominance to competing for market shares, as well as shifting the nature of competition from systems to components and from features-competition to price-competition.[11]

3.1.3 Standards as public goods

"Public goods" are goods and services that benefit all consumers but that tend to be undersupplied by private sector investors because they are "nonrival" *and* "nonexcludable." A good or service is nonrival if the marginal cost of providing it to an additional consumer is zero, that is, if consumption of the good or service by one consumer does not diminish its availability for other consumers.[12] A good or service is nonexcludable if people cannot be excluded from consuming it. The classic example of a pure public good is national defense. Once it is provided, all citizens enjoy it. The transparent and international process by which FIPS-197 was developed, selected, and made freely available to the public is similar to national defense in this regard. The AES is both a nonrival and a nonexcludable public good.[13]

While public goods and services are provided by public and private institutions, it is likely that the government will play an important

---

[11]Ibid., p. 228.

[12]Classic examples of nonrival goods are highways (during low traffic volume) and lighthouses. Since the highway and the lighthouse already exist, the marginal cost of providing these services to additional consumers (drivers in the first instance, ship pilots in the second instance) is zero.

[13]As a practical matter, it is more common to find goods and services that have one "public good" characteristic but not the other so that the "publicness" of public goods is best considered as falling on a spectrum of publicness, ranging from pure public goods (national defense) to pure private commodities. Even industry-driven consensus standards developed and published in the United States by standards development organizations (SDOs) may not be *pure* public goods to the extent that access to them comes at cost that could effectively exclude some potential users. In any event, SDOs produce standards with considerable public goods content. On the imagined spectrum of publicness, FIPS-197 is located closer to the pure public goods end of the spectrum than FIPS-140-2. To the extent that fees are paid to obtain certification, FIPS-140-2 would appear to be somewhat less non-excludable than FIPS-197. However, modes of operation specifications *are* freely available, even if a certificate is not. FIPS-140-2 is closer to a pure public good on the spectrum of publicness than would be if the specifications were not freely available.

role in providing them at a level commensurate with societal welfare. The publicness characteristics of public goods make the role of public institutions (or other forms of collective action, such as standards consortia) instrumentally important. Private-for-profit organizations invest to generate a return on their investment in excess of opportunity costs. If these returns cannot be realized, it makes little sense to make the investment. Public organizations, on the other hand, can take a broader view. If they can demonstrate a broad benefit to society of an investment in public goods and services, that investment (on the part of the public) may be justifiable because the total benefits (summed across all beneficiaries) may exceed the social cost by a sufficient amount to justify the public investment.[14]

The know-how and services provided by NIST's CSD — such as FIPS-197 and FIPS-140-2, as well as a library of "Special Publications" concerned with modes of operation and various aspects of computer security assessment — are public goods in the sense just described. NIST's AES program has provided cryptographic infrastructure technology (that arguably would be underprovided by the private sector acting alone) to improve the economic performance of cryptographic goods and services.

3.1.4 FIPS as market failure-mitigating tools

When the buyers in markets realize the benefits of their purchases, and the suppliers face the costs of the resources that they use for production, if markets have an adequate number of buyers and sellers engaged in a competitive process, the signals provided by market prices to the market's participants are generally believed to enable the market mechanism to allocate scarce resources efficiently. Market failures are instances where prices do not adequately reflect the value of resources and consequently resources are not efficiently allocated. Instead, too

---

[14]From an economic perspective, there is a threshold return on an investment established by the cost of public borrowing. The cost of public borrowing is addressed in Office of Management and Budget Circular A-94. See Albert Link and John Scott, *Public Accountability: Evaluating Technology-Based Institutions*, Kluwer Academic Publishers, 1998, pp. 17–21.

many of society's resources are used in some activities, while too few are used in others.

In the context of investments in new technologies, there are many types of barriers to technology development and commercialization that can cause too few resources to be allocated to those activities, leading to underinvestment by the private sector. Some of the underinvestment is routinely mitigated by government programs and/or collaborations with industry and university partners.[15] Generally speaking, these barriers to technology development cause risk and uncertainty to rise and reduce the ability of private firms to capture sufficient investment returns to justify the private investments in socially valuable technology. If such barriers are not mitigated they can lead to market failures by underinvestment in socially valuable technology.[16] If the various barriers to technology development and commercialization are reduced, allowing private firms to realize higher returns and lower risk on their investments, private investment more closely approaches its social value. Thus, government initiatives that reduce barriers to technology development, and thus stimulate a socially desirable level of investment, function as market failure mitigating policy tools. FIPS are an example of market failure mitigating policy tools.

Barriers to cryptographic technology development and commercialization were quite high when NIST's AES program was initially launched in the mid-1990s. According to a contemporaneous 1996 National Research Council report, the United States was "in the midst

---

[15]Tassey, *Economics of R&D*, op. cit., especially Chapter 5, "Rationales for Public Sector R&D Policies," and Chapter 6, "Alternative Policy Mechanisms," pp. 81–130.

[16]The following categories of technology development and commercialization barriers have been identified as precipitating market failures: externalities, information-sharing difficulties, recognition, long time to market, incompatibility, and inadequate infra-technology. For a fuller discussion, with additional examples, see, David Leech, Albert Link, and John Scott, *The Economics of a Technology-Based Service Sector*, NIST Planning Report, No. 98-2, U.S. Department of Commerce, January 1998, especially pp. 27–36; Gregory Tassey, *The Economics of R&D Policy*, Quorum Books, 1997 (especially Chapter 5, "Rationales for Public Sector R&D Policies," pp. 82–100). For a discussion of the "market failure" modes that these barriers may precipitate, see John Roberts, *The Modern Firm*, Oxford University Press, 2004; and Oliver Williamson, *The Economic Institutions of Capitalism*, Free Press, 1985.

of a policy crisis, unable to develop a consensus about cryptography policy."[17] The dimensions of the crisis included the following:

1. Export restrictions reduced the private sector incentive to invest in R&D for a new algorithm.

2. Industry could not agree on what stronger encryption looked like, and what was actually possible to achieve.

3. There was lack of demand for stronger encryption in the broader market and uncertainty about future demand. (In the mid-1990s, only a minority of technical experts and cryptographers understood the growing need for information security in the Internet-based society that was in its infancy.)

4. The cost of cryptographic products was high. (Prior to AES development, much of encryption was performed by separate standalone chips and hardware boxes. The cost of incorporating encryption hardware was higher than today, where encryption is often performed from a set of program files.)

5. Lack of certification/verification/validation of encryption implementations stronger than DES or TDES led to consumer uncertainty about the value and actual performance of encryption.

6. Lack of interoperability between different computer systems and software, and lack of encryption standards to bring industry together, was leading to a fragmented-market situation with "everyone rolling their own" encryption protocols.

7. Industry and consumer distrust occurred because of concerns that encryption standards from the government were designed with a capability for the government to access private communications. As a result, many computer and automated systems lacked encryption protections.[18]

---

[17] *Cryptography's Role in Securing the Information Society*, National Research Council, 1996, p. xvi.
[18] Ibid.

While all of the above would have contributed to commercial uncertainty, the technical uncertainty associated with cryptography has always been high. In the words of a current cryptographer, it is "fiendishly difficult" to develop an encryption algorithm, so much so that, "even seasoned experts design systems that are broken a few years later."[19] The situation around 1995 seemed setup for market failure where encryption technology was concerned. The development of the FIPS-197 on a not-for-profit, open, royalty free basis pulled the market away from this impasse and supported the following decades' tremendous growth of computer and Internet products and services.

3.1.5   FIPS as infra-technology

NIST's role in the economy has been conceptualized as providing "infrastructure technology," or "infra-technology." Just as roads and bridges are frequently referred to as the infrastructure of regional and national economies — because they reduce the cost of getting from here to there and, thereby, expand the geographic boundaries of markets for goods and services — infra-technology serves a similar function in the realm of R&D processes, product development, and product commercialization.[20]

AES and the CAVP and CMVP — FIPS-197 and FIPS-140-2 — are quintessential infra-technologies. The process by which AES was developed is a textbook case of government-industry cooperative investment and has been touted as a shining example for developing similar standards.[21] FIPS-197 can be understood as a cryptographic *product standard* (inasmuch as source code is a product): a set of specifications

---

[19]Ferguson, op. cit., p. 13.

[20]The term "infra-technology" was coined to describe the "technical tools" that are ubiquitous in a high-tech economy and provide substantive foundation for many standards. Infra-technologies include measurement and test methods, standard artifacts (such as standard references materials or weights and measures artifacts), scientific and engineering reference databases, process models, and the technical basis for both physical and functional interfaces between the components of systems technologies. See, Gregory Tassey, *The Economics of R&D Policy*, Quorum Books, 1997.

[21]Ferguson *et al.*, op. cit., p. 321: "AES Is the Shining Example of How to Standardize Security Systems."

to which some or all elements of products under its jurisdiction must conform. In the same way, FIPS-140-2 can be understood as a crypto-graphic *non-product standard*. Together they represent public goods of significant economic value that likely would not have been forthcoming from the private sector alone. As explained in Section 3.1.4, risk and uncertainty associated with the networked nature of encryption system, the high public goods content of effective encryption algorithms, the sheer technical difficulty of designing sufficiently strong algorithms, and the uncertainty surrounding the international market for encryption products would have reduced the ability of private firms, acting alone, to capture sufficient investment returns to justify the private investments in socially valuable technology on par with what NIST provided.

As infra-technological product and non-product standards, FIPS-197 and FIPS-140-2 had the potential to significantly reduce costs across the three major stages of technology-based economic activity: R&D, production, and commercialization.[22] They exhibit three of the four functions typical of standards in knowledge-intensive industries:

(1) Enable variety reduction among designs and functions of product elements (FIPS-197);

(2) Specify quality and reliability of product and process technologies (FIPS-140-2); and

(3) Provide performance-related information on characteristics of resources and actual products and processes (FIPS-140-2).[23]

These functions, operating across the stages of product development and commercialization, are largely responsible for creating the cost avoidance benefits and economic impacts described and estimated in the following chapters of this monograph.

---

[22]Tassey, 2017, op. cit., p. 247.

[23]Ibid., p. 228. Tassey defines the fourth function to be the assurance of interoperability for hardware and software components of technology-based systems. Neither FIPS-197 nor FIPS-140-2 assures interoperability of two or more encryption systems except to the extent that the systems, independent of the certification process, employ AES-certified hardware and software modules. FIPS-140-2 certification does not certify the encryptions systems that utilize certified modules.

3.2 Encryption systems in an industrial context

3.2.1 Encryption systems value chain

The value chain depicted in Figure 3.1 is a snapshot of the complex process by which many economic actors contribute their ingredients to product and service integrators further down the chain and, ultimately, to intermediate and final users of encryption services. Value chains are conventionally thought of in terms of the upstream sources of basic technology (cryptographic algorithms) and the value added as they move downstream through the tiers of the value chain toward intermediate and final users.[24]

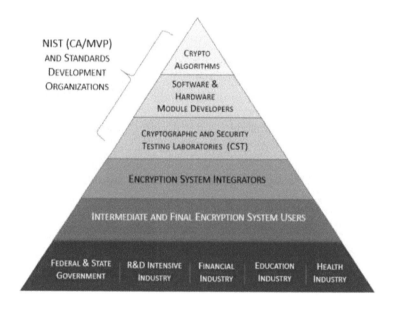

Figure 3.1: The encryption system value chain.

---

[24]It has become commonplace to discuss information-intensive and networked industries in terms of an "ecosystem" of which they understand themselves to be a part. See, for example, M. Iansiti and R. Levien, *The Keystone Advantage: What the New Dynamics of Business Ecosystems Mean for Strategy, Innovations, and Sustainability*, Harvard Business School Press, 2004; and David Evans *et al.*, *Invisible Engines: How Software Platforms Drive Innovation and Transform Industries*, MIT Press, 2008. However, knowledgeable industry representatives assert that cryptographic software and hardware developers and integrators *do not* tend to use the language

Cryptographic algorithm developers are specially trained or experienced mathematicians. The Bureau of Labor statistics reports 40,300 employed mathematicians in 2016.[25] Only a very small fraction of these was likely employed in the development of cryptographic algorithms. Reportedly, most cryptographers work for the NSA, other government agencies, or in academia. Commercial cryptographers are likely few in number and probably primarily employed by large multi-national corporations.[26]

Cryptographic module developers are surely the employers of some cryptographic algorithm developers. The only systematic source of information concerning module developers is NIST's CMVP, which allows for commercial companies to submit encryption products for formal testing by CST labs. If approved, the product becomes eligible for sale to the Federal Government. As of December 2017, the companies holding the largest number of active *AES hardware validation* certificates included Cisco Systems, Thales e-Security, Motorola Solutions, SafeNet, and Brocade Communications Systems. Companies holding the largest number of active *AES software validation* certificates included Microsoft, Apple, RSA, Red Hat, and Cisco Systems.

Cryptographic and Security Testing (CST) laboratories are authorized by NIST, through the NVLAP to perform the CAVP and CMVP testing. There are currently 21 CST labs, including several international locations.[27] For most labs, such testing is 5% or less of their annual revenues.[28] Certificates are generally good for five years before re-evaluation is necessary. Industry participants estimated the average cost to obtain a CMVP certificate generally ranges from $50,000 to $100,000. This cost includes the testing lab fees, NIST cost recovery fees, internal testing, application preparation, and often consulting fees.

Encryption system integrators incorporate validated modules into larger computer, computer peripheral, network equipment, and software

---

of ecosystems to describe the dynamics of their industry, so the more conventional description of a vertical value chain is used here.

[25] https://www.bls.gov/ooh/math/mathematicians-and-statisticians.htm.

[26] https://www.bls.gov/careeroutlook/2012/fall/art01.pdf.

[27] https://www-s.nist.gov/niws/index.cfm?event=directory.results.

[28] Estimate based on email exchanges with testing lab representatives.

systems. By and large they are thought to be the same companies that apply for cryptographic hardware and software module validations, but it is the modules alone, not the higher-order equipment and systems, that are validated and certified. For example, the Microsoft Windows operating system contains a cryptographic module library with reference code for numerous encryption algorithms. It is this library file and the modes of access to it within the software that is submitted for CMVP testing, not the overall operating system product.

Intermediate and final encryption system users represent a wide, and possibly widening, swath of industries. It is generally believed that Federal and state agencies, banking and finance, and health-related industries have been the heaviest users of encryption systems in the past. Federal agencies must secure confidential data with AES or TDES. A canvas of state agency Information Security Offices found that most are FIPS-140-2 compliant for at least some of their departments. Survey responses were received from across the economic landscape, beyond those historically identified with encryption, including: agriculture; construction; manufacturing; retail trade; transportation and warehousing; information; real estate rental and leasing; professional, scientific, and technical services; management services; waste management; educational services; and arts and entertainment.[29]

NIST and Standards Organizations interact with several layers of the value chain. NIST provides direction for the CAVP and CMVP. These two programs aid private sector companies in selling regulatory compliant products to the Federal Government. Passing modules receive a certificate of FIPS compliance and are listed on NIST's website allowing Federal entities to consult the list for FIPS compliant IT products.

Standards bodies dealing with encryption matters include the International Standards Organization (ISO), the Internet Engineering Task

---

[29] A dimension of the value chain that is not clearly depicted here includes products that are not "encryption systems" as we have defined them but which incorporate security algorithms or subsystems, for example, road vehicle security systems and digital cinema security systems. Encryption technology likely plays a role in any use scenario involving securing data from hacking or other threats. All such "every-day" examples of encryption applications fall into the "final encryption system user" tier.

Force (IETF), Institute of Electrical and Electronics Engineers (IEEE), and the American National Standards Institute (ANSI). Since the issuance of FIPS-197, numerous standards have been revised or developed which reference FIPS-197 as a "normative reference," that is, *indispensable* to the application of the standard.[30] The strongest concentration of normative references occurs between 2008 and 2010, when numerous standards were issued concerning telecommunications and networking security, road vehicle security, digital cinema data security, and home security. These are indicative of the widespread introduction of digital platforms across the world at the end of the first decade of the 2000s. Touchscreen application-enabled phones were released, the concept of Internet of Things emerged, and "big data" and data-driven analytics were becoming popular.[31] The first digital camera filmed movies won Oscars.[32] Broadband Internet brought lightning fast banking, chat, shopping, and gaming to many American homes. Since 2011, the majority of encryption standards have focused on telecommunication networks. As the technology for fast Internet improves, the need to maintain equally fast and secure capabilities is paramount.[33] Banking and financial markets, doctor visits and health

---

[30]Standards referencing AES issued between 2008 and 2010 include: ISO/IEC ISO/IEC 26430-3: Digital cinema (D-cinema) operations — Part 3: Generic extra-theater message format; ISO/TS 24534-5: Automatic Vehicle and Equipment Identification; ISO/IEC 24767-2: Home network security, communication protocol for middleware; ISO/IEC 19772: Information technology — Security techniques — Authenticated encryption; ISO/IEC 18033-4: Information technology — Security techniques — Encryption algorithms — Part 4: Stream ciphers; ISO/IEC 24771: MAC/PHY standard for ad hoc wireless network to support QoS in an industrial work environment; ISO/IEC 11889: Trusted Platform Modules; ISO/IEC 18013-3: Information technology — Personal identification — ISO-compliant driving license; ISO/IEC 14543-5-1: Information technology — Home electronic system (HES) architecture; ISO/IEC 13141: Electronic fee collection — Localization augmentation communication for autonomous systems; ISO/IEC 13157-2: Information technology — Telecommunications and information exchange between systems — NFC Security — Part 2: NFC-SEC cryptography standard using ECDH and AES.

[31]The iPhone was first released in 2007.

[32]*Slumdog Millionaire* was the first all-digital film to win an Oscar in 2009.

[33]Seven additional AES related ISO standards were identified between 2011 and 2017, four of which are related to telecommunications or streaming protocols. They include: ISO/IEC 16504:2011 — Information technology — Telecommunications and information exchange between systems; ISO/IEC 23001-7:2015: Information

data, proprietary intellectual property and private information, car and phone navigation systems, shopping purchases and browsing habits, gaming and chat sessions — all rely on the Internet to some extent and involve data that people and companies wish to protect from unauthorized access and use.

Figure 3.2 tracks the industries covered by AES-dependent standards over the years, that is, standards containing a normative reference to AES, FIPS-197. In the figure, the year is based on first year the dependent standard was released.[34] Many financial industry-related

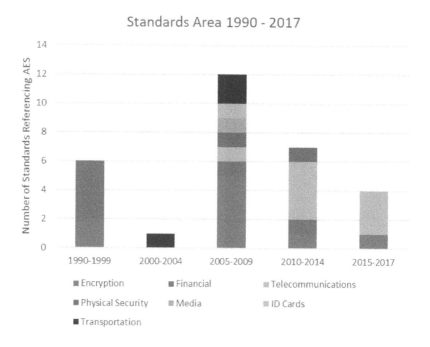

Figure 3.2: AES-dependent standards.

---

technology — MPEG systems technologies; ISO/IEC DIS 23009-4:2013: Information technology — Dynamic adaptive streaming over HTTP (DASH); ISO/IEC 13157-3:2016: Information technology — Telecommunications and information exchange between systems.

[34]In many cases we could only ascertain the initial year released and the most recent revision. Thus, we could not precisely determine when the post-AES standard revision was released in most cases.

standards were released pre-AES and were subsequently revised in years following the 2001 publication of FIPS-197. The chart captures the general development in AES-dependent standards over time. Developing a new standard generally takes two to five years; thus, the period of 2000 to 2004, immediately after the release of FIPS-197, sees only one AES-dependent standard in transportation issued, while the subsequent period from 2005 to 2009 has the largest concentration of new AES-dependent standards. It is probable that a majority of the standards issued in the 2005 to 2009 period were under development in the preceding period from 2002 onward.

3.2.2 Encryption system market size and composition

In 1986, a Congressional Office of Technology Assessment study reporting on what it called the "Government Information Revolution" provided that, "despite the fairly widespread agency use of electronic dissemination of [Federal] Government information, such use is still largely in the formative stages."[35] By 1991, the National Academy of Sciences, worrying about the risk posed to data confidentiality, concluded:

> Whereas the market in 1980 was dominated by commercial computer and communications systems with *no security features*, the market in 1990 includes a significant number of systems that offer discretionary access control and a growing number from both major and niche vendors with both discretionary and mandatory access control, which provides significant protections against breaches of confidentiality. (Italics added.)[36]

Attempting to characterize more precisely the size and shape of the market for cryptography, the authors of an influential report by the National Research Council (1996) found what this paper's investigation of the market for encryption systems found:

---

[35] *Federal Government Information Technology: Management, Security, and Congressional Oversight*, Congress of the United States, Office of Technology Assessment, February 1986, p. 145.

[36] *Computers at Risk*, National Academy of Sciences, 1991, p. 143.

The committee was unable to determine the size of the information technology market directly affected by export controls on encryption... the floor of such estimates — a few hundred million dollars per year — is not a trivial sum. Furthermore, all trends point to growth in this number, growth that may well be very large and nonlinear in the near future. ....Most sales of information technology products with encryption capabilities are integrated products.... the market for cryptography is... not well defined when integrated products with encryption capabilities are involved.[37]

The situation today is similar. Respected market analysts can clearly identify market segments of software and network equipment and estimate their market value and share distribution, but they are unable to estimate the security-related portions. What market size and share distribution information is readily available is of questionable veracity and cannot be ascertained without purchasing the questionable data.[38] The companies identified as the predominant market participants in the readily available estimates of encryption-related software and hardware markets are among those identified as the top five CMVP certificate holders (listed in the discussion earlier of cryptographic module developers).

This chapter developed an economic analysis framework by placing the AES program in its broader economic and industry context. From an economic perspective, high and rising switching costs and the subsequent lock-in effect of networked systems can act as barriers to the development and adoption of more efficient and secure encryption systems. This chapter explained that standardization, generally, is a method of reducing the costs associated with the lack of network

---

[37] *Cryptography's Role in Securing the Information Society*, National Research Council, 1996, pp. 148–49.

[38] This is a problem referred to as "the information paradox" whereby the value for the purchaser is not known until the information is reviewed, and the provider is unwilling to allow review prior to purchase. Kenneth Arrow, "Economic Welfare and the Allocation of Resources for Invention," p. 615, in *The Rate and Direction of Inventive Activity: Economic and Social Factors*, National Bureau of Economic Research, Princeton University Press, 1962.

interoperability and incompatibility. It discussed how the public goods nature of standards causes them to function as tools for mitigating technology development barriers that lead to market failures. FIPS-197 and FIPS-140-2 were further characterized as infra-technological standards with the potential to generate significant cost-avoidance benefits. Finally, this chapter introduced the encryption system value chain, from cryptography developer to intermediate and final users of encryption systems.

Chapter 4 will build on the economic and industry analysis framework to identify specific cost-avoidance benefits enabled by the AES program, map out a plausible counterfactual scenario, and identify the categories of potential beneficiaries.

4

Economic Impact Assessment Approach

4.1 Survey strategy

The central question posed by the survey for this economic impact assessment was, "What would it have cost industry, acting without NIST support, to develop and adopt a strong successor to the operative encryption standard (DES, FIPS-46) in the mid-1990s as DES was coming to the end of its useful life as a secure symmetric block cipher?"[1]

The answer to the basic question requires answers to the following questions:

> Would the private sector, acting alone, have developed a standardized strong and efficient replacement for DES sooner or later than the year 2000 (the year the *Rijndael* cryptographic algorithm was selected as the AES)? If not, why not?

---

[1]This question entails what is described as the "counterfactual method," the appropriate method for assessing the economic impacts of publicly funded, publicly performed investments. See, Albert Link and John Scott, *Public Goods, Public Gains: Calculating the Social Benefits of Public R&D*, Oxford University Press, 2011, pp. 31–32.

If the private sector would not have developed a standardized strong and efficient replacement for DES sooner than 2000, what would have been the consequences? In other words, what kinds of costs and risks would have been incurred by developers and users of encryption systems in the absence of a widely accepted replacement for DES in 2000, and for how long would those costs have been incurred?

What jargon or technical terms and units of measure are used by the community of cryptography developers and users to describe and discuss the costs and risks associated with relatively weak encryption?

These and derivative questions were posed by the authors in their reading of published literature concerning the AES, and in interviews and email exchanges with members of NIST's original AES competition program team and several experienced industry representatives and cryptographers. Some of the latter had developed algorithms for the AES 1997 competition. These scoping interviews attempted to clarify the timeline for the paper, establish important stages in the AES program and their dates, ascertain possible motivations for the program and the problems it addressed, and to differentiate the many areas of economic benefits (cost avoidance) practitioners hoped to achieve.

In parallel, a plausible counterfactual scenario of what might have happened in the absence of NIST was developed. This further clarified the nature of various cost avoidance benefits enabled by the AES program. Characterization of cost avoidance benefits and the counterfactual scenario provided a framework for developing hypotheses about the broader economic impact of AES, and finally, survey questions.

4.1.1   Seven broad categories of cost-avoidance benefits identified

The retrospective impact of NIST's AES program is primarily the function of the costs avoided by having a central, trusted body take the initiative and bear some of the costs of the development of a stronger, computationally more efficient and flexible replacement of DES and the interim TDES.

In the absence of NIST's leadership, the evolution of a sufficiently strong and efficient encryption technology and its implementation as AES would have been significantly retarded. From the supply side of the market, the costs of related R&D, production, and commercialization would have been higher.[2]

The survey questions were designed to help quantify several categories of potential avoided costs identified in scoping interviews and historical research conducted by the authors. Large-scale encryption systems such as in-house data centers and cloud computing services were the organizational focus of the survey directed at encryption system consumers. Multiple servers and communication equipment are typically co-located in data centers due to their environmental requirements, ease of maintenance, and physical security needs. It was assumed that management personnel associated with data centers or reporting to Chief Information Security Officers (CISOs) would have ready access to information concerning the performance and costs associated with encryption systems.[3] Senior technical managers were the focus of survey questions directed at cryptographic module developers and encryption system integrators.

Survey questions were developed to obtain estimates concerning hypothesized areas of avoided costs including the following:

1. Avoided costs of slower processing speed

A test of encryption speeds between TDES and AES determined that AES was approximately six times faster than TDES on current hardware. It was assumed that, all else held constant, slower processing speeds would require additional resources. The survey questions asked respondents to quantify the additional resources.

---

[2] Ibid.

[3] Personal communication with data center industry analysts, Peter Christy (12-5-17 through 3-13-18) and Andy Lawrence (12-6-17 through 12-8-17). See, also, *A Peep into Data Center Economics: Analyzing Challenges & Opportunities*, Wipro Technologies, 2011; and Luiz Andre Barroso, Jimmy Clidaras, and Urs Holzle, *The Datacenter as a Computer: An Introduction to the Design of Warehouse-Scale Machines*, Second Edition, 2013 (1st edition, 2009), Google, Inc.

2. Interoperability costs avoided

To tackle interoperability costs, it was assumed that in the absence of AES, developers and integrators would have to duplicate efforts writing code and performing maintenance on multiple algorithms. It was hypothesized that without AES, there would have been a fragmented market with multiple algorithms in use within or across different industrial sectors. These benefits would accrue to consumers and producers of encryption systems, and respondents were asked to quantify such benefits.

3. Breach costs avoided

Between 1996 and 2016, there was no indication that AES was successfully attacked and broken by brute force attacks or cryptanalysis. DES, on the other hand, was susceptible to attack, and by association TDES was susceptible, too. It follows that organizations moving to AES would receive intangible benefits by reducing the likelihood of successful cryptanalysis attacks. Moreover, absent AES, there would have been more diversity among the strong encryption algorithms in use by networks both during and after the time of the AES competition and the selection of the new standard. Such multiplicity of algorithms would have caused additional complexity and potential lapses enabling hackers to breach security systems. In the survey questions, encryption system users were asked to disclose the average annual number of cyberattacks against encrypted data over the past five years, as well as describe their understanding of the relationship between multiple encryption algorithms, resulting interoperability issues, and the risk of successful breaches.

4. Pre-acquisition costs avoided

In the face of fragmented markets, the resulting interoperability issues and an absence of consensus standards, organizations purchasing encryption systems would be forced to engage in a host of pre-acquisition activities that raise costs. These activities typically include product search costs, qualification-testing costs, and acceptance costs. Survey respondents were asked to estimate any increases in these and related costs in the counterfactual absence of AES.

5. Standards development costs avoided

There are multiple industry organizations that develop encryption standards including the ISO, IEEE, IETF, and ANSI. These organizations rely on volunteered time from experts working in industry and government. Since NIST took on the task of evaluating algorithms and producing a standard, the standards organizations and commercial entities received a benefit of reduced costs for standards development. Currently, these standards organizations have issued guidance that reference FIPS-197 and FIPS-140-2. In the absence of NIST's work, it was hypothesized that these organizations would have incurred more labor hours and longer delays to produce standards and guidance in this area. Survey respondents were asked for estimates of these hypothesized effects on their organizations.

6. Lost sales and profits avoided

Over and above the costs avoided in the development of AES-dependent standards, sales of standardized products and services would also have been affected. Survey respondents were asked to estimate how market growth would have been affected absent AES.

7. Hardware and software module quality degradation avoided

The validation process associated with FIPS-140-2 compliance adds value to cryptographic modules and systems. In the absence of the AES program, both the avoided costs for producers to assure the quality of their products and the added confidence afforded consumers of encryption systems would have been foregone. Survey respondents were asked to estimate these benefits.

4.1.2   The counterfactual scenario

The counterfactual scenario is used as a means for pulling background research and interview information together and conceptualizing the economic benefits of the AES program by imagining what would have happened had it been postponed or had never occurred. A time series of the estimated annual sum of costs avoided is interpreted as the economic benefits of the AES program, and those benefits are then compared with the program's actual costs.

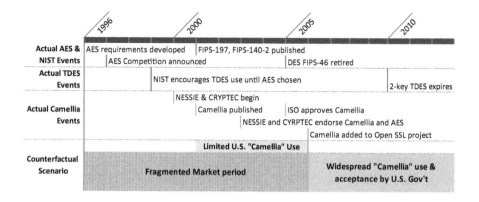

Figure 4.1: AES program timeline and counterfactual scenario.

Figure 4.1 graphically depicts some main events of the AES program (top panel). The period under investigation begins in 1996, the year NIST's CSD began to organize internally for the AES competition the following year. Without NIST, what would have happened from this point on?

Camellia, a modern algorithm with technical similarities to AES (third panel), was released in 2000 and endorsed by the ISO in 2005.[4] Camellia's development timeline synchronized well with industry estimates of standards development times.

Due to the infra-technological nature of the AES program, the benefits of the AES program were expected to span the product life cycle of cryptographic products and services, from R&D to commercialization.[5] The "absent NIST" counterfactual (bottom panel) has three

---

[4]Camellia is a 128-bit symmetric block cipher very similar in operation to AES. It was developed jointly by the Japanese companies Mitsubishi Electric and Nippon Telegraph and Telephone (NTT) and released in 2000. In 2005, the ISO/IEC accepted it as an encryption standard. It was endorsed by the European NESSIE and Japanese CRYPTEC committees as a recommended cipher alongside AES. Some U.S. technology experts suggested that Camellia was developed as a Japanese national version of AES and suggest that Camellia would not have existed without the NIST competition and the resulting AES. Although Camellia as a national algorithm would not have been accepted "as is" by the U.S. Government or U.S. standards bodies, it is plausible that Camellia or something like it would have become the foundation for a TDES replacement algorithm along a similar timeline.

[5]Tassey, 2017, op. cit., p. 228.

components: market fragmentation, consensus standardization in the absence of AES, and the TDES option. It was hypothesized that market fragmentation would have ensued from 1997 to 2004 while industry and standards organizations sought a strong unified alternative to DES and TDES.

The hypothesized market fragmentation which industry representatives described in the 1990s would have extended through approximately 2005. This period would have had multiple, post-TDES strong and efficient solutions emerging.[6] Minimally five, possibly more, of the original 15 algorithms submitted to the AES competition could have been pursued even though it is known, as a result of the analysis performed during the AES competition, that some of the 15 had serious flaws and would not have been successfully developed. These solutions would have emerged in response to an increased need for security driven by increasing risk of attacks and security breaches, as well as in response to Federal, state, and international regulations passed since 1995.[7] It is anticipated that even after 2005, if there had not been an AES competition and the new standard had not been widely accepted, problems associated with a multiplicity of strong encryption algorithms would have been more prevalent.

In pre-survey interviews some industry representatives suggested that none of the NIST competition algorithms would have been

---

[6]Marco Giarratana, "The Birth of a New Industry: Entry by Start-Ups and the Drivers of Firm Growth: The Case of Encryption Software," *Research Policy* Vol. 33, 2004, pp. 787–806; Marco Giarratana and Andrea Fosfuri, "Product Strategies and Survival in Schumpeterian Environments: Evidence from the U.S. Security Software Industry," *Organization Studies*, Vol. 28, No. 06, pp. 909–929, 2007; Andrea Fosfuri and Marco Giarratana, "Resource Partitioning and Strategies in Markets For Technology," *Strategic Organization*, (forthcoming).

[7]The European Union's Data Protection Directive (officially Directive 95/46/EC) adopted in 1995; the Health Insurance Portability and Accountability Act of 1996 (HIPAA; Pub. L. 104–191, 110 Stat. 1936, enacted August 21, 1996); the Federal Information Security Management Act of 2002 ("FISMA", 44 U.S.C. §3541, *et seq.*); the Sarbanes–Oxley Act of 2002 (Pub. L. 107–204, 116 Stat. 745, enacted July 30, 2002); Directive 2002/58/EC of the European Parliament and of the Council of 12 July 2002; the Health Information Technology for Economic and Clinical Health Act, abbreviated HITECH Act, was enacted under Title XIII of the American Recovery and Reinvestment Act of 2009 (Pub. L. 111–5); and the Payment Card Industry Data Security Standard (PCI DSS), with multiple releases, 2004–2016.

developed without the AES competition. Instead, they posited that existing block ciphers such as Blowfish, RC5, and IDEA would have come into widespread use. The NIST competition uniquely forced industry and academia to produce innovative 128-bit block ciphers with 128-bit and greater keys, which previously was thought too difficult and computationally onerous to be practical. Although there would no doubt have been multiple alternatives to TDES, the evolution of a much stronger 128-bit cipher would have taken a more wandering path, and it is difficult to pinpoint when it may have appeared.

Market fragmentation generally heralds higher interoperability costs, as well as increased risk and complexity of supporting multiple non-standardized algorithms. Cryptography experts warn that, "complexity is the worst enemy of security." It was hypothesized that added complexity would increase risk for developers and users and, in turn, increase the probability of failed product roll-outs by developers and of breach losses by users.

In a possible version of the market fragmentation counterfactual, failed attempts to quickly fill the void in the absence of NIST's initiative might have materialized. If serious attacks had occurred during a period of market fragmentation, subject matter experts have offered historical examples of retrospectively imprudent attempts to advance insufficiently considered standards with serious cost consequences.[8]

One significant aspect of this period is that these alternatives represent what are called "national algorithms." NIST's competition was global and the winner was European. As such, AES has met with little adoption resistance in Europe and other parts of the globe. Lack of a global competition coupled with the proprietary development of "American" algorithms by U.S. entities, the widespread cross-border use of one U.S.-selected algorithm would likely never have emerged.

In summary, estimates of the size and temporal distribution of cost avoidance benefits from the AES program were the primary focus of

---

[8]Examples provided by subject matter experts include the first and second versions of the *de facto* Secure Sockets Layer (SSL), intended to provide communications security over computer networks, and Wired Equivalent Privacy (WEP), a security algorithm introduced as part of the original IEEE 802.11 Wi-Fi standard ratified in 1997.

the survey. The nine-year fragmented market period is hypothetically characterized by competing domestic algorithms, slower diffusion of encryption technology, and limited international adoption. Even beyond the nine-year period, the problems associated with the complexity of multiple strong encryption algorithms in the absence of AES would have been expected. Government and commercial enterprises using encryption would not only have had to support more, possibly less efficient, domestic algorithms, they would likely be supporting separate algorithms for different sectors of the economy, and for each country (or block of countries such as the European Union). Such fragmentation would have led to higher development, validation, testing, maintenance, and technical support costs, as well as increased the complexity and vulnerability of information systems.

Lack of U.S. leadership in this area would have impaired the competitive advantage of U.S. information technology companies, who were already struggling in the 1990s with restrictive export policies and the international perception that U.S. information technology products were subpar. The U.S. information technology sector relies in part on government regulation and pronouncements to determine the direction of R&D efforts. e-Commerce, the Internet, streaming services, and cloud computing all would have experienced significant interoperability issues that would have retarded U.S. technology advancements. It is likely that, in this scenario, U.S. companies would not have dominated global technology business as they do today, or that Internet-based goods and services would have been in such pervasive domestic use.

4.1.3 Segmenting the survey recipient population

Two broad groups of likely beneficiaries of FIPS-197 include *consumers* of encryption systems and *developers* of encryption systems.

Encryption system consumers were further distinguished into two groups: *public sector* and *private sector* consumers of information encryption systems. The range of encryption system hardware and software choices available to each group is different, and therefore the consequences of their choices have different economic effects. Broadly, public sector consumers are limited by FIPS and other regulations, whereas private sector consumers are less restricted in their options.

For the purposes of the survey, public sector consumers include the CISOs of Federal agencies, the 50 states, and one territory. Private sector consumers include the CISOs, Chief Information Officers (CIOs), and/or data center managers of private sector firms that use encryption in their routine operations. These entities have historically been concentrated in the R&D-intensive manufacturing sector, and in the financial, medical, and e-commerce service sectors. Professional cybersecurity associations whose members include private sector CISOs were invited to participate in the AES economic impacts survey.

As a result, the final survey instrument contained sets of survey questions for three distinct groups of potential respondents:

1. Government consumers — This group included Federal and state Chief Information Officers and any other government IT managers who were members of organizations distributing the survey. The survey for this group was 13 questions.

2. Private consumers — This group included companies that use a product containing encryption in their data centers or other services, but do not actually make or develop encryption products. Survey recipients included CISOs, CIOs, and other individuals with managerial or oversight responsibilities around encryption choices. The survey for this group was 26 questions.

3. Private integrators — This group included companies that develop and produce encryption hardware or software. It also included private academicians, independent encryption validation consultants, and independent cryptographers. The survey for this group was 20 questions.

4.2   Survey execution

4.2.1   Survey instrument development

Based on communications with the cryptographic community, extensive background research, and the hypothesized benefits and counterfactual scenario, survey questions were formulated and iteratively improved with an eye to what could likely be collected from each of three different groups of beneficiaries: private sector consumers, public sector consumers, and developers and integrators of cryptographic hardware and software.

The full survey instrument is available on request.

4.2.2 Survey distribution

A professional online platform (research.net hosted by Survey Monkey) was selected to make distribution and survey completion simpler and more streamlined. This online approach greatly simplified the logistics of contacting and reminding the survey population to complete the survey. It also simplified data aggregation and analysis after the survey closed. Section 5 details the number of responses, their type, and industry affiliations.

Direct survey contacts were contacted by email via the Survey Monkey platform. Selected members of participating organizations were contacted by email or through a form of communication deemed appropriate by them (e.g., periodic newsletters or announcements). Invitations to participate included a prefatory note from Donna Dodson, NIST's Chief Cybersecurity Advisor and Director of the National Cybersecurity Center of Excellence (NCCoE).

The open survey period ran from February 26, 2018 through April 9, 2018.

4.2.3 Direct and indirect access to survey recipients

A list of current Federal CIO's was obtained from NIST. The National Association of State Chief Information Officers (NASCIO) provided the point of contact for the CIOs or CISO's of 50 states and one territory.

NIST publishes validated certificate holders on its website. The list of AES CMVP holders was downloaded and analyzed to identify the entities holding the most active certificates and the most certificates overall, both active and historical. Emails and phone calls were made to the listed contacts to establish contact. Many of these contacts turned out to be technical managers who had a good understanding of how AES functioned, but had reduced visibility concerning business decisions such as the size of the IT budget and what portion of it was dedicated to encryption-related activities and equipment. Nonetheless, these individuals provided good insights into the forces at play during the development and roll out of AES.

A number of organizations with interests in information security were contacted. The following organizations agreed to invite selected members of their organization to participate in the survey with the stipulation that the authors would not have direct access to members' contact information:

- ANSI's Accredited Standards Committee X9 (ASC X9, Inc.)

- The Anti-Phishing Working Group (APWG)

- College of Healthcare Information Management Executives (CHIME)

- Cryptographic Module User Forum (CMUF)

- Common Criteria User Forum (CCUF)

- Executive Women's Forum on Information Security (EWF)

- Information Systems Audit and Control Association (ISACA)

- Information Systems Security Association (ISSA)

- IEEE's LAN/MAN Standards Committee (IEEE 802)

- National Council of Information Sharing and Analysis Centers (NCI ISAC)

- National Technology Security Coalition (NTSC).

Following an initial invitation, all organizations sent at least one reminder message to their members during the survey period.

5

Survey Results and Findings

5.1 Survey results

The survey contained three sets of questions for three distinct groups:
1) public sector consumers; 2) private sector consumers; and 3) cryptographic module producers, developers, and integrators. Survey responses
were received from 169 respondents, of which 74 provided sufficient
quantifiable information to allow for direct estimates of economic
benefits. The 74 respondents consisted of the following:

- **Private sector consumers (demand side) — 33 respondents**

    o Representing eight industry sectors: construction, manufac-
    turing, retail trade, information technology, finance, scientific
    and technical services, health care, and arts and entertain-
    ment.

- **Public sector consumers (demand side) — four respondents**

    o Federal Government — civilian and military agencies.

    o State, local, and tribal Governments.

- **Cryptographic module producers, developers, and integrators (supply side) — 37 respondents**
  - Private-sector producers/developers of cryptographic modules.
  - Private-sector integrators — use externally made cryptographic modules to build other products.
  - Academic or Independent Cryptographers.
  - Cryptographic validation testing consultants (these individuals work closely with numerous private-sector producers, developers, and integrators).

Figure 5.1 shows in pie wedges the number of respondents of each type and its percentage of the 74 respondents, private-sector consumers were the largest group of respondents, followed by private-sector producer/developers. The rate of response from Federal and state entities was considerably lower than anticipated.

The additional 95 respondents can be characterized by type of respondent (private consumer, private producer/developer, private integrator, public consumer, academic or independent cryptographer, and cryptographic testing consultants) and their industrial classification category(ies). They answered various survey questions that could not be used to directly estimate their organizations' economic benefits. However, as explained fully in Section 5.3, information provided by all 169 respondents is used to extrapolate (from the economic benefits reported by the 74 respondents with directly quantifiable responses) the benefits of the 95 survey respondents who did not provide direct information about their benefits.

5.2   Introduction to survey findings

The survey findings are both qualitative and quantitative. The qualitative findings are matters of interest that can be used to verify or reject the pre-survey counterfactual hypotheses. The quantitative findings are used in calculations of the annual cost-avoidance benefits. Table 5.1

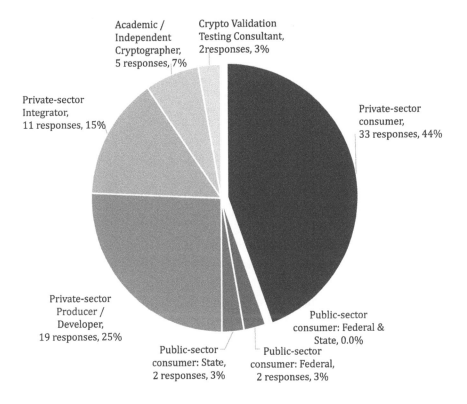

Figure 5.1: Survey results: 74 respondents reporting quantifiable benefits.

summarizes pre-survey hypotheses and indicates whether each finding has been assessed quantitatively, qualitatively, or both.

5.3   Qualitative discussion of survey findings

5.3.1   AES-stimulated cryptographic research and development

The evidence that the AES program stimulated significant cryptographic research and development that would not have been undertaken as early, or on such a scale, is largely a matter of the economic logic of public goods (discussed in Section 3.1.3), the history of how the AES competition was implemented, and anecdotal evidence. Some private sector observers at the time recall paying close attention to the results of the AES competition as they unfolded and adjusting

Table 5.1: Anticipated survey findings.

Pre-survey hypothesis	Qualitative	Quantitative
AES-stimulated research & development.	X	X
Desire for key strength greater than TDES was prevalent.	X	
High switching costs postponed transition to AES.	X	
Absent AES, interoperability would have declined, and system complexity would have increased.	X	X
Absent AES, the risk of data breaches would have increased.		X
CMVP certifications reduce procurement and sales-related costs.		X
CMVP reduces the cost of module production and increased buyers' willingness to pay a premium.		X
AES increased standard development process efficiency and improved time-to-market for dependent products.		X

their product and service offerings accordingly, in some cases before the formal announcement of the competition winner.

The core process of requesting AES submissions, analyzing them, announcing and analyzing finalists, and selecting a winner ran from 1997 to 2000. Industry, government and academic sectors of the cryptographic community made analytical contributions, including concentrated attempts to break the submitted ciphers. The person–years of analytical support across the cryptographic community are thought to have been very large.[1] The benefits from the R&D stimulated by the

---

[1]One estimate put the contribution of NSA alone at 13 person–years of analysis.

AES program began accruing no earlier than 1998, after the competition was well under way, but before the formal announcement of a winner.

The relatively small quantity of benefits attributable to the early R&D stimulated by the AES program and the timing of those benefits are interpreted as evidence of cryptographic R&D stimulation. The benefits fall into three categories:

- Avoided costs of interoperability testing,

- Foregone "willingness to pay" benefits enjoyed by buyers of validated products,

- Costs avoided by producers due to implementation errors discovered in preparation for module validation.[2]

For the period 1998 to 2000 only, it is estimated that these benefits together account for approximately $5.8 million (2017 dollars) in R&D cost avoidance benefits.[3]

5.3.2 Desire for key strength > TDES was not a common sentiment

By the mid-1990s the cryptographic community — academia, government, and industry — knew that DES was vulnerable to attack, that TDES was therefore at increased risk, and that TDES had technical constraints in terms of its relatively small block size. Based on this, it was hypothesized that alternatives to TDES would be quickly adopted and that AES (or an equivalently strong and efficient block cipher) would have emerged as the block cipher of choice. Survey results did not confirm this supposition.

---

[2]The survey instrument did not ask for R&D estimates. Companies offering FIPS-140 approved products from 1998 to 2000, or before, were assumed to be deeply engaged in following, or participating in, the AES competition and its results and thereby enjoyed R&D-related benefit captured in the three benefits categories available to respondents.

[3]The economic calculations and survey data supporting this amount are described in Section 5.4.

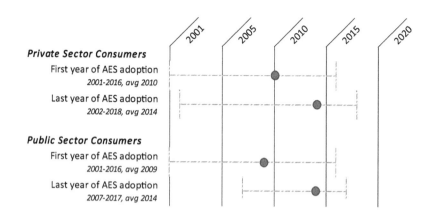

Figure 5.2: Survey results: first and last years of AES adoption: range and average.

The survey questions for all recipients inquired about the first and last years in which their data centers adopted AES.[4] Respondents provided the ranges and averages shown in the graph below. As illustrated in Figure 5.2, although both private sector and public sector consumers have the same date range for first year adoption, on average public sector consumers adopted one year earlier than their private sector counterparts. For the last year of adoption, on average the private and public sectors' date of last AES adoption is the same.

Survey results indicate that AES tended to be first adopted by the private sector around eight years after it took effect as the Federal standard stronger than TDES. For private-sector consumers of encryption systems, AES was finally being fully adopted by data centers only in the last few years, with an average year of adoption in 2014, more than a decade after AES was published as FIPS-197.[5] The presurvey impression that an encryption algorithm stronger than TDES was popular seems to have been incorrect. Its perceived popularity did not result in a rush to transition.

---

[4]Seventy-nine private sector consumers of encryption systems provided the year in which their data centers first adopted AES. Seventy-six private sector consumers of encryption systems provided the year in which the last of its data centers adopted AES. Seven Federal agencies respondents provided first and last AES adoption dates.

[5]Seventy-six private sector consumers responded to this question. Responses ranged from 2003 to 2017 with a median of 2016 and a mode of 2017.

5.3.3 The transition to AES was postponed by high switching costs

The authors anticipated that some users would resist the shift from TDES to AES because of a variety of switching costs, especially, but not exclusively, associated with necessary security system hardware and software upgrades or replacements.[6] Economic theory concerning information system supply and demand (Section 3.1), as well as the case study of the transition from DES/TDES to AES encryption systems in the banking and finance sector (Appendix A), indicates that high switching costs among users and suppliers are likely to have played an important role in stifling the adoption of AES-based encryption systems.

As indicated in Figure 5.3, survey results were mixed with regard to this issue, but the overall argument presented here affirms it. Public and private sector consumers were asked Yes/No questions regarding aspects of transitioning an encryption system from DES/TDES to AES. Private sector respondents were split on the existence of high switching costs as well as on whether they faced internal or external push-back in making the transition to AES.[7] More than three-quarters believed that the transition required significant hardware or software upgrades, enough to merit scheduled work. As discussed in Section 5.3.2, respondents were slower to adopt AES than anticipated; 76% of 86 private sector encryption system consumer survey respondents affirmed that encryption system suppliers were responsive. It could be that over time the significance of switching costs declined when compared to other issues data center managers confronted.

Private-sector consumer respondents were asked to identify the industry sector to which their organizations belonged according to the two-digit North American Industry Classification System (NAICS). Isolating answers about switching costs of those 41 respondents identifying themselves with the banking and finance sector (NAICS 52), 41% affirmed high switching costs as a factor, while 59% rejected switching

---

[6]N. Ferguson *et al.*, op. cit., p. 59: "If you have to be backward compatible or are locked into a 64-bit block size by other parts of the systems, [TDES] is still your best choice."

[7]Eighty-seven private-sector respondents answered these questions.

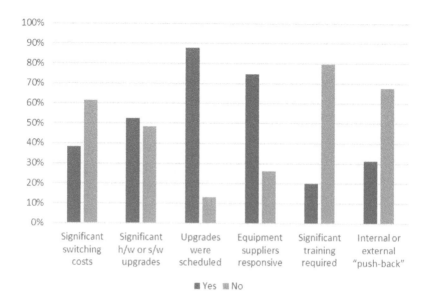

Figure 5.3: Survey results: Transitioning from DES/TDES to AES.

costs as a significant factor in AES-based encryption system adoption. Of those affirming high switching costs, their average number of years between first and last adoption of AES was 5.2 compared to a 4.4 year spread for those rejecting high switching costs. We can therefore deduce that for those who perceived higher switching costs for AES system adoption, full AES adoption took longer.

5.3.4   Absent AES, system complexity and risk increase

Cryptography experts assert that, "complexity is the worst enemy of security."[8] It stands to reason that "absent AES," the increased complexity of ensuring interoperability, given an increase in the number of different strong encryption algorithms in use by different encryption systems, would increase risk for encryption system users. As indicated in Figure 5.4, by and large, these expectations were confirmed. Of the 59 encryption system users and producers who provided historical speculations about an absent AES market scenario, almost half (49%)

---

[8]Ferguson *et al.*, op. cit., p. 37.

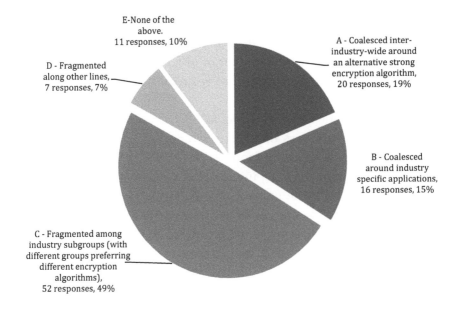

Figure 5.4: Survey results: Respondents' most likely "absent AES" scenario.

indicated that they believed option (C): the market would have fragmented among industry subgroups with different groups preferring
different encryption algorithms. Options C, B, and D entail some
significant degree of fragmentation, indicating that 71% of respondents
(C, 49% + B, 15% + D, 7%) believed that market fragmentation (and
therefore increased complexity of ensuring interoperability) was likely
absent AES. Only 19% believed that an inter-industry-wide alternative
strong encryption algorithm (Option A) would have emerged. In the
counterfactual absence of AES, the most frequently suggested alternative
by survey respondents was Twofish.[9]

Encryption system users were further asked how an increase in the
number of different encryption networks affects the costs of maintaining
interoperability. Of those responding to the question, 80% believed

---

[9]While Twofish was a response to the AES competition, it is reasonable to assume
that a version of it would have emerged as demand grew for algorithms with greater
key strength than TDES.

that costs rise linearly or exponentially as the number of different encryption networks increases. Additionally, respondents were asked if security risks increase as the number of different encryption networks increases. Again, 80% concurred that security risks would increase in this circumstance.

Finally, respondents were asked for the average number of data breaches (due to malware or hacking) reported to Federal or state authorities in the five-year period of 2013–2017. This response was used, in combination with the information regarding the relationship between breaches and the number of different encryption algorithms in use, to approximate the expected number of data breaches that respondents would have experienced absent AES. Out of all encryption system user respondents, 48% reported zero breaches for the period and 52% reported a positive number of breaches. The average number of breaches for all respondents was two breaches during the five-year period. For those reporting a positive average number of breaches, the average was four breaches over the five-year period.

5.4   Quantitative findings

Section 5.4.1 describes the beneficiaries (survey respondents) and explains how benefits from NIST's program were estimated for 74 respondents to the survey and concludes with a time series of those benefits summed across all benefit categories annually, 1998–2017. Section 5.4.2 extrapolates the benefits for the sample of respondents to larger groups of beneficiaries in two stages, first to all 169 survey respondents, and then to the industries that all survey respondents represent. Section 5.5 describes NIST's costs for the AES program. The time series of costs and benefits described are used to calculate the overall economic impact metrics in Section 6.

5.4.1   Review of 74 survey respondents

As discussed in Section 5.1, of 169 survey responses, only 74 provided sufficient quantifiable information to allow for direct economic impact calculations. Thirty-three respondents represented private sector consumers of encryption systems from eight industrial sectors; four public sector consumers of encryption systems representing Federal and state agencies; and 37 suppliers (producers, developers, integrators, and independent cryptographers and consultants) of cryptographic modules and encryption systems. Each of those 74 respondents typically did not provide enough information to quantify *all* of the types of benefits addressed with the survey; they often acknowledged that the benefits existed but did not attempt to provide the answers to the survey questions that would have allowed a quantitative estimate for each and every benefit category.

5.4.2 Directly quantifiable benefits and methodology for 74 respondents

The categories of measurable benefits gathered from the 74 respondents are summarized in Table 5.2. The table is followed by a discussion of the specific types of data gathered for each proposed benefit category and the methodology used for calculating those benefits.

Benefits of faster AES processing speed

Private and public sector consumers provided either known or estimated quantities for the following:

1. Their AES adoption date;

2. Their 2017 encryption budget;

3. Their 2017 encryption processing hours;

4. The annual growth rate in encryption processing hours since the adoption of AES; and

5. The multiple of the encryption budget needed to accommodate slower processing time in the counterfactual absence of AES.

Information provided by 24 consumers of cryptographic services allowed calculating the counterfactual avoided costs of encrypted data processing in 2017 constant dollars over the years since the respondent adopted AES.

Table 5.2: Quantifiable survey topics posed to three groups.

| Survey questions regarding | Demand side | | Supply side |
	Private sector consumers	Public sector consumers	Cryptographic integrators
Benefits of faster AES processing speed	x	x	
Interoperability costs avoided	x		
Interoperability testing costs avoided			x
Breach costs avoided	x		
Avoided pre-acquisition costs for encryption hardware and software	x		
Standards development costs avoided	x	x	x
Avoided lost profits from standards delay			x
Customers' benefits from validation testing			x
Producers' benefits from CA/MVP assisting implementation-error corrections			x
Benefits from the expansion of international markets			x

Interoperability costs avoided

Private sector consumers of encryption systems provided estimates of the following:

1. Their AES adoption date;

2. Their 2017 encryption budget;

3. Their total 2017 encryption processing hours;

4. The annual growth rate in encryption processing hours since the adoption of AES; and

5. The increase in encryption processing hours needed to deal with interoperability issues across different encryption algorithms in the counterfactual absence of AES.

Based on the information provided, the avoided interoperability costs for the counterfactual scenario were calculated for 16 private sector consumers of encryption systems using the conservative assumption that entities would have only one additional algorithm and encryption network to deal with — a particularly conservative assumption because interoperability issues are typically described as increasing exponentially with the number of different algorithms.

Interoperability testing costs avoided

Producers, developers, and integrators of encryption products were asked to quantify the following:

1. Their 2017 person–hours for interoperability testing across encryption modules and encryption containing products;

2. The full 2017 compensation (salary and benefits) for requisite personnel;

3. The multiple of the person–hours required for interoperability testing absent AES; and

4. The estimated annual growth rates for the sales of encryption hardware and/or software since the first AES-containing product was sold.

Based on the information provided, a time series for the avoided costs of interoperability testing was estimated for 30 cryptographic suppliers.

Breach costs avoided

Private sector consumers provided either known or estimated quantities for the following:

1. The average number of breaches per year over the last five years; and

2. The relationship between number of breaches and number of interoperating encryption networks.

Most respondents that provided breach data also said that breaches would increase exponentially or linearly with the number of different encryption networks.[10,11] Since none of the respondents were able to provide an estimate of the exponent for exponential relation, the avoided costs were calculated using the conservative assumption of a linear relationship and also the conservative assumption of just one more encryption network — i.e., one more different encryption algorithm — to deal with in the counterfactual absence of AES. The cost of a breach in the United States in nominal U.S. dollars for each of the years 2006 through 2016 was obtained from the Ponemon Institute.[12] The breach costs for 2003, 2004, 2005, and 2017 were extrapolated using ordinary least squares.[13] The nominal breach costs

---

[10]Twenty-nine of 36 private sector encryption system consumers responding concurred with the following statement: "As the number (n) of interoperating encryption networks increases, complexity increases, and as complexity increases (holding everything else constant) the risk of security breaches (with the number of breaches = s) increases." Twenty-four of 27 concurring and responding to a question about the average number of breaches due to malware or hacking believe that the number of breaches (s) rises linearly or exponentially as the number (n) of interoperating encryption networks increases.

[11]Denoting the number of breaches with y and the number of networks as x, an exponential relationship would mean $y = ax^b$, while a linear relationship would mean $y = a + bx$, where a and b are constants.

[12]All breach cost estimates are based on the average total cost of a data breach for U.S. companies as reported in annual studies by The Ponemon Institute. Breach costs for 2006–2011 are reported in annual editions of *Annual Study: Cost of a Data Breach*. Breach costs for 2012–2016 are reported in annual editions of *Cost of Data Breach Study: Global Analysis* (2013–2017).

[13]Separate regression lines were fitted for the years 2006 through 2010 and the years 2011 through 2016. The fits of the regression lines were good. For the earlier period the $R^2 = 0.8233$, $F(1,3) = 13.97$, probability of a greater $F = 0.0334$. For the later period, $R^2 = 0.9409$, $F(1,4) = 63.68$, probability of a greater $F = 0.0013$.

were converted to 2017 constant dollars using the chain-type price index for GDP.[14]

Avoided pre-acquisition costs for encryption hardware and software

Assuming that AES did not exist and some level of a proliferation of encryption algorithms occurred as a result, pre-acquisition costs (e.g., product search costs, qualification testing costs, and acceptance costs) for encryption hardware and software would probably have increased. Private consumer respondents were asked to quantify or estimate the following:

1. The number of full time personnel in 2017 dedicated to encryption software and hardware pre-acquisition activities;

2. The multiple of those personnel that would have been required in 2017 in the counterfactual absence of AES; and

3. The full compensation (salary and benefits) in 2017 of a qualified full-time person performing these activities.

The information reported by 21 private sector consumers of encryption systems allowed calculating the avoided pre-acquisition costs in the counterfactual scenario absent AES.

Avoided standards development costs

All respondents were provided with a list of standards from the ISO, IETF, IEEE, and ANSI which contain normative references to AES. All categories of respondents were asked to do the following:

1. Identify the standards they had worked on; and

2. Assuming the counterfactual absence of AES, estimate the number of

    a. additional hours that their personnel would have devoted to the standards work; and

[14]The chain-type price index for gross domestic product (GDP) was obtained from Table B.3, "Quantity and price indexes for gross domestic product, and percent changes, 1967–2017", p. 536, *Economic Report of the President*, February 2018, Government Publishing Office, and on the Internet at www.gpo.gov/erp.

    b. additional months that the particular standards would have been delayed.

The information provided by 17 suppliers and 19 consumers of encryption systems allowed the calculation of counterfactual standards development costs avoided and the placement of the avoided costs in the appropriate years when the extra standards development work would have occurred.

Avoided lost profits from standards delay

Additional benefits exist for the supply-side respondents in the form of avoided lost profits from standards delay. Cryptographic suppliers were additionally asked to estimate the following:

1. The probable average delay in months, for the standards on which they had worked, in the counterfactual absence of AES; and

2. The probable average lost revenue per each month's delay.

The assumption is that a company's operations would have continued and the costs to produce products would have remained the same, but the sales would have been slowed. Sales would likely have slowed while products pending standards were withheld from the market or became outdated sitting on shelves. Hence, the lost revenues during a month's delay translate to a loss in profits for that month. Given the actual release dates for the standards and the number of months they would have been delayed in the counterfactual scenario, the benefit of the estimated avoided lost profits could be added to the time series of AES benefits for 10 cryptographic suppliers.

Customers' benefits from validation testing

Supply-side respondents (cryptographic producers, developers, and integrators) provided information about their customers' benefits from validation testing as reflected in the prices paid by the buyers of encryption hardware and software. FIPS-140-2 validation testing is valuable to module producers because it provides valuable assurances to buyers that producers' encryption hardware and software conform to high standards of cryptographic security. These assurances mean that buyers are willing to pay more for the validated product. Respondents estimated the following:

1. The value of these validation-testing assurances, as a percent of module average price ranges that they provided for 2017;

2. The years in which their sales of AES-related FIPS validated hardware and/or software began; and

3. The growth rates for sales of the FIPS validated encryption hardware and/or software.

From the information provided by 26 supply-side respondents, a time series was constructed of the lost value that was avoided by buyers of the hardware or software modules, given that validation testing increases buyers' willingness to pay.

Producers' benefits from CA/MVP-assisting implementation-error corrections

FIPS-140-2 validation testing is valuable to cryptographic hardware and software module producers because it uncovers or confirms implementation errors that module producers would otherwise need to correct, for example, by sending technicians to test and fix bugs that were not fixed prior to module deployment. At a minimum, the value of FIPS validation testing is the cost to producers of correcting errors found (or confirmed) in the validation process. That is because the validation testing in any year is an investment in the new product or products being tested. The present discounted value, to the developer and producer, of the future returns on that investment during the year must be at least equal to the testing cost (so that benefits at least equal the costs). Thus, a lower bound on the value in a representative year is provided by a respondent's costs of correcting implementation errors found or confirmed in the validation process. Cryptographic producers provided estimates, across all modules validated by their organization in a representative year, of the following:

1. The total number of person–hours dedicated to correcting implementation errors found or confirmed in the validation process; and

2. The average annual full-time compensation (salary plus benefits) of personnel with the appropriate capability to perform the necessary tasks.

With the information provided by 27 producers, a time series of the avoided lost value was constructed to provide estimates of average annual benefits over the years since sales of the AES-related FIPS-validated products began. Some suppliers reported selling FIPS-validated products beginning in the period before the availability of knowledge about the strong encryption standards emerged during the AES competition; for those respondents the benefits of implementation-error correction were not begun until the AES era was underway starting in 2001.

Benefits from expansion of international markets

The development and promulgation of AES increased worldwide demand for products and services incorporating strong symmetric block encryption. Cryptographic suppliers provided estimates of the following:

1. Information about the 2017 sales of encryption-containing modules;

2. The years in which their sales of AES-related FIPS validated hardware and/or software began;

3. The average annual growth rate for their strong cryptographic hardware and software module sales;

4. The average annual sales growth rate that would have occurred in the absence of AES; and

5. The AES-related standards that supported the respondent's sales.

The foregoing information, provided by 15 suppliers, allowed estimation of the difference between the actual time series for sales and what the time series would have been in the absence of AES. Beginning at the release time for the AES-related standards supporting the sales, and holding the producer's costs constant,[15] the time series of the difference between actual sales growth and counterfactual retarded sales growth provided a time series of benefits. These benefits were avoided lost profits — lost profits that would have resulted as sales growth in the counterfactual scenario slowed due to the loss of the AES effect on international standards and the expansion of international markets for cryptographic products and services.

For each of the 74 survey respondents reporting benefits from any of the areas described above in a given year, benefits were summed and accumulated across all respondents. Table 5.3 shows the time series of AES benefits for all respondents in a given year, in 2017 constant dollars, 1998 to 2017.

The benefits calculated for the 74 respondents in Table 5.3 are conservative totals for many reasons. Prominent among them are the underestimates for the supply-side respondents of buyers' benefits from validation testing and benefits from expansion of international markets. Note that the benefits before 2002 reflect the benefits of the AES competition, that is, the benefits for the R&D cost avoidance by crypto-graphic suppliers — producers, developers, integrators, academics, and consultants. The years with pronounced jumps in benefits reflect years with a large number of new beneficiaries in the counterfactual scenario because of their AES adoption dates (for consumer organizations in the sample) or because of the beginning of FIPS-validated sales (for producer organizations in the sample).

In Section 5.4.3, these benefits are extrapolated to larger samples (described in Section 5.1), and when the extrapolation is complete, we extrapolate from the cumulated present values of benefits in 2017 for the 74 observations to the analogous cumulative benefits for the larger samples. Thus, our extrapolations will not provide the individual, yearly amounts of each category of benefits over the period from 1996 through

---

[15]This is a sensible first-order estimation, given the way the production of encryption products and services works with the on-boarding of new clients to use the products developed. The time series of costs for the supplier stays the same, but the time series for a portion of the sales is shifted into the future periods.

Table 5.3: AES benefits for 74 survey respondents.

Year	Total benefit* (Constant 2017 dollars)
1998	1,841,514
1999	1,934,932
2000	2,046,763
2001	7,688,332
2002	15,920,284
2003	34,271,978
2004	46,318,887
2005	67,439,960
2006	50,839,308
2007	82,014,903
2008	80,076,964
2009	91,392,576
2010	175,000,000
2011	189,500,000
2012	184,100,000
2013	199,900,000
2014	296,400,000
2015	321,700,000
2016	370,400,000
2017	399,400,000

*For 74 respondents who provided sufficiently quantifiable responses.

2017, but their total, cumulated at the social rate of return to have their present value in 2017 dollars.

5.4.3 Extrapolation of benefits to larger samples

As illustrated in Figure 5.5, the extrapolation of benefits from the 74 respondents discussed in Section 5.4.2 to larger samples takes place in the following two stages:

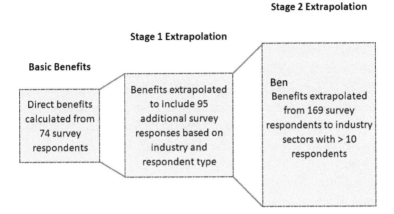

Figure 5.5: Extrapolation of benefits in two stages.

- First, the benefits based on the 74 respondents reported in the section above are extrapolated to an additional 95 survey respondents. Those 95 respondents did not provide information from which cost avoidance benefits could be directly estimated, but they did provide enough information to allow estimation of their benefits by using an estimated model of the benefits for the 74 respondents with direct information about benefits;

- Second, the benefits are extrapolated for the industrial sectors to which the 169 survey respondents belong.

Briefly, a first stage extrapolation begins with the estimates from the 74 survey respondents, discussed in Section 5.4.2, and assumes that an additional 95 survey respondents who identified themselves by industry sector (two-digit NAICS code), and type of respondent (private consumer, private producer/developer, private integrator, public consumer, academic or independent cryptographer, and cryptographic testing consultants), would have provided statistically similar responses to those provided by respondents of the same type and in the same industry sector (a full explanation of this approach is explained in Appendix D). For each of the 74 respondents, the present value of all the benefits (in 2017 constant dollars) they reported between 1998 and 2017 was calculated as of 2017 (hereafter referred to as an organization's "cumulative benefits"). Then, the question is statistically posed: "Do the cumulative benefits of each of the 74 survey respondents vary significantly on the basis of their industry sector and/or type of respondent?" The answer is "yes;" statistically speaking, the cumulative benefits can be explained with a model that has industry sector and type of respondent as the explanatory variables. That estimated model is used to predict the cumulative benefits of the additional 95 survey respondents.

Accordingly, summing the benefits for the 169 individuals that responded to the survey — 74 with information of at least some of their quantitative benefits and another 95 with sufficient categorizing information (respondent type and industry) used in our estimated model of benefits — the cumulative benefits for all 169 survey respondents is $8,899,000,000.[16]

A second-stage extrapolation used the cumulative benefits of the 169 survey respondents discussed above, and information about the industrial sector to which the respondents belong, to estimate the benefits of the AES program for large sectors of the U.S. economy represented by survey respondents. Briefly, the employment size of each respondent's organization (in some cases reported and in other cases estimated) was used to estimate the proportion of the sector's employment taken by the respondents belonging to that industrial sector. (This procedure was only used where the number (n) of the 169 respondents belonging to an industrial sector was 10 or greater.) Benefits were extrapolated for the following sectors: NAICS 31-33 — Manufacturing ($n = 45$), NAICS 51 — Information ($n = 47$), NAICS 52 — Finance and insurance ($n = 42$), NAICS 54 — Professional, scientific, and technical services ($n = 41$), NAICS 61 — Educational services ($n = 12$), NAICS 62 — Health care and social assistance ($n = 13$), and NAICS 92 — Public administration ($n = 16$).

Each industry sector is assigned all the cumulative benefits for the *n*survey respondents in that sector (n of 169) as described in the

---

[16]The economic impact metrics for this benefit stream are presented in Section 6, Table 6.3.

first-stage extrapolation above. For example, looking at the Manufacturing row of Table 5.4, the cumulative benefits (1998–2017) for
the 45 respondents reporting in that industry sector are estimated
to be $907,000,000 (column 4). The total employment reported or
estimated for those 45 survey respondents is approximately 1.8 million
(column 3) and the total employment for the manufacturing sector in
2017 is reported as approximately 12.3 million (column 5). Using the
proportion of total industry sector employment represented by the 45
survey respondents belonging to that sector (column 6), we estimate
cumulative benefits for the manufacturing sector as a whole (column
7) by dividing the proportion of total industry sector employment
represented by the 45 survey respondents (column 6) into the value of
the cumulative benefits estimated for the 45 survey respondents. Thus,
(the n respondents' benefits in the sector)/(proportion of the sector's
employment taken by the n respondents) = (benefits for the sector).

Summing the benefits for the all sectors shown in Table 5.4, column 7,
gives the total extrapolated AES benefits for the sectors with 10 or
more respondents. Those total benefits equal $250,600,000,000. These
estimated benefits are calculated *as if* annual benefits had been invested
at the OMB-specified rate of 7% and cumulated over two decades. Since
benefits were not estimated for the sectors of the economy where the
survey had fewer than 10 respondents, the sum of the estimated benefits
for the sectors shown in the table is a lower bound of the total benefits
for the economy.

5.5   NIST's costs for the AES program

NIST provided the total AES program annual costs from the incipiency
of the program in 1996 through 2017. Those costs, for total compensation
of labor and the overhead costs, included costs for the research, the
standardization activities, and the updating of modes of operation
and the development of new modes of operation to accommodate the
increased block size of the AES algorithm. Also included were the costs
of AES-related validation work. The annual costs were provided in
2012 constant dollars, and the costs were converted to 2017 constant

Table 5.4: Extrapolation of AES benefits to the economy.[17]

(1) Sector (industry classification, NAICS)	(2) n	(3) Total 2017 employment for the n respondents	(4) Total $PVbnft2017_{sector}$ for the n respondents (2017 dollars)	(5) Total 2017 employment for the sector*	(6) Proportion of sector employment for the n respondents	(7) Estimated $PVbnft2017$ for the sector (2017 dollars)
Manufacturing (31–33)	45	1,773,633	907,000,000	12,299,600	0.1442	6,290,000,000
Information (51)	47	1,624,431	1,090,000,000	2,800,500	0.5801	1,879,000,000
Finance and Insurance (52)	42	544,272	2,690,000,000	5,857,390	0.09292	28,950,000,000
Professional, scientific, and technical services (54)	41	394,052	2,030,000,000	8,850,270	0.04452	45,600,000,000
Educational Services (61)	12	48,756	87,600,000	13,042,580	0.003738	23,430,000,000
Health care and social assistance (62)	13	90,154	555,000,000	20,208,050	0.004461	124,400,000,000
Public administration (NAICS 92, OES 99)	16	181,127	376,000,000	9,661,980	0.01875	20,050,000,000

*United States Department of Labor, Bureau of Labor Statistics, Occupational Employment Statistics, "May 2017 National Industry-Specific Occupational Employment and Wage Estimates," https://www.bls.gov/oes/current/oessrci.htm, accessed May 4, 2018.

---

[17]The economic impact metrics for this estimate's benefit stream are presented in Section 6, Table 6.3.

Table 5.5: Time series of NIST's AES program costs.

	Year	NIST's total annual AES program costs (Constant 2017 Dollars)
AES competition and development	1996	$ 349,272
	1997	2,655,110
	1998	2,655,110
	1999	2,655,110
	2000	2,655,110
	2001	2,655,110
	2002	4,216,052
	2003	3,016,240
	2004	3,182,252
	2005	3,335,327
	2006	2,563,480
	2007	2,836,214
	2008	2,497,722
	2009	2,352,193
	2010	2,401,781
	2011	2,436,276
	2012	2,482,630
	2013	2,521,438
	2014	2,626,004
	2015	2,626,004
	2016	2,677,748
	2017	2,730,570

dollars.[18] Table 5.5 shows the time series of NIST's annual costs for the AES program.

---

[18]The annual costs were converted to 2017 constant dollars using the using the chain-type price index for gross domestic product (GDP), Table B.3, "Quantity and price indexes for gross domestic product, and percent changes, 1967–2017", p. 536, *Economic Report of the President*, February 2018. Government Printing Office, and on the Internet at www.gpo.gov/erp.

6

Economic Impact of the AES Program, 1996–2017

6.1 Economic impact metrics

The present value, at the onset of the AES program in 1996, of the time series of NIST's annual costs for the AES program is \$30,633,590 in 2017 constant dollars.[1] The time series of AES benefits for only the 74 survey respondents at the onset of the AES program in 1966 (from Table 5.3) is \$875,133,112 in 2017 constant dollars.[2]

---

[1] The present value of NIST's costs is the amount that would have to be invested, at the beginning of the investment project and earning the social required rate of return of 7% per year (as used in the previous NIST evaluation studies — see Albert N. Link and John T. Scott, *The Theory and Practice of Public-Sector R&D Economic Impact Analysis*, NIST Planning Report #11-1, January 2012, National Institute of Standards and Technology, U.S. Department of Commerce; the 7% social discount rate was introduced in Office of Management and Budget (OMB), Circular no A-94: Guidelines and discount rates for benefit-cost analysis of Federal programs, Washington D.C.: Government Printing Office, 1992), in order to release in each year an amount equal to the cost in that year. Thus, the present value of the costs is $\sum_{t=0}^{T} COST_t/(1.07)^t$, where $T = 2017 - 1996 = 21$.

[2] The present value of the benefits for our 74 respondents is that amount that if invested at 7% per annum at the beginning of the investment project would release in each year an amount equal to the benefits in that year. Thus, the present value of the benefits is $\sum_{t=0}^{T} benefit_t/(1.07)^t$, where $T = 2017 - 1996 = 21$.

Table 6.1: Evaluation metrics for the 74 respondents.

Benefit-to-cost ratio	28.6
Net present value	$844,500,000
Internal rate of return	0.807 or 80.7%

Table 6.2: Extrapolated evaluation metrics for the 169 survey respondents.

Benefit-to-cost ratio	70.2
Net present value	$8,772,000,000
Alternative internal rate of return*	0.310 or 31.0%

*For comparative purposes, the alternative internal rate of return for the 74 survey respondents presented in Table 6.1 is 25.5%.

Table 6.1 summarizes conventional evaluation metrics using only the benefits for the 74 respondents. Based solely on the benefits reported for the 74 respondents, the present value of the benefits divided by the present value of the costs, the benefit-to-cost ratio, is 28.57; the surplus of benefits over the costs, the net present value, for NIST's AES program is $844,499,522. The internal rate of return for the AES program — the rate at which NIST's investments in the AES program is growing — is 0.807 or 80.7%.[3]

Table 6.2 summarizes conventional evaluation metrics using the extrapolated benefits for 169 respondents (the Stage 1 extrapolation described in Section 5.4.3). The present value in 2017 of NIST's costs over the years from 1996 through 2017, Present Value NIST Costs$_{2017}$, is $126,800,000.[4] Using the estimated AES benefits for the sample of 169 organizations, the benefit-to-cost ratio, Benefit$_{2017}$/Cost$_{2017}$, is $8,899,000,000/$126,800,000 = 70.18. The net present value, Net Present

---

[3]The internal rate of return is the interest rate that discounts the stream of benefits to the present value of the stream of costs. Thus, it is r such that $\sum_{t=0}^{T} COST_t/(1+r)^t = \sum_{t=0}^{T} benefit_t/(1+r)^t$.

[4]Thus, the present value in 2017 of NIST's AES costs provided in Table 1 is $\sum_{t=1996}^{2017} COST_t \times (1.07)^{2017-t}$.

Table 6.3: Evaluation metrics for the extrapolation of 169 survey responses to selected sectors of the U.S. Economy.[5]

Benefit-to-cost ratio	1976.3
(Net present value)$_{2017}$	$250,473,200,000
Alternative internal rate of return*	53.6%

*For comparative purposes, the alternative internal rate of return for the 74 survey respondents presented in Table 6.1 is 25.5%.

Value$_{2017}$, is $8,772,000,000. For reasons explained in Appendix C (Understanding the Alternative IRR), an "alternative internal rate of return" of 0.310 or 31.0% is computed rather than the conventional internal rate of return.[6]

Table 6.3 summarizes the metrics for the extrapolation to the economy-wide effect of NIST's investments. Summing the benefits for the all sectors shown in column 7 of Table 5.4 (Section 5.4.3) gives the total extrapolated AES benefits for the sectors with 10 or more respondents. Those total benefits equal $250,600,000,000. Recall that these are benefits invested and cumulated over two decades. In the sense that benefits for the sectors of the economy where we have fewer than 10 respondents are not estimated, the sum of the estimated benefits for the sectors shown in the table are a lower bound of the total benefits for the economy. The cumulated present value amount as of 2017 of NIST's costs was defined and discussed in the earlier discussion. We then have a lower-bound estimate of the AES benefit-to-cost ratio for the economy: the sum of the sector benefits in Table 5.4, column 7 (from Section 5.4.3) divided by the present value in 2017 of NIST's

---

[5]Notes: (Present value in 2017 of AES economy-wide benefits cumulated from 1998)$_{\text{lower bound}}$ = $250,600,000,000. (Present value in 2017 of NIST's AES costs cumulated from 1996) = $126,800,000. (AES Economy-wide Benefit-to-Cost Ratio)$_{2017, \text{lower bound}}$ = 1976.3. (AES Economy-wide Net Present Value)$_{2017, \text{lower bound}}$ = $250,473,200,000. Alternative internal rate of return = 0.536 or 53.6%; it is the solution r to the equation: $(30,633,590)*(1+r)^{21} = 250,600,000,000$.

[6]This alternative internal rate of return is the solution r to the equation: $(30,633,590)*(1+r)^{21} = 8,899,000,000$.

costs for the AES program over the years from 1996 through 2017; the ratio is $250,600,000,000/$126,800,000 = 1976.34$. A lower-bound AES economy-wide alternative internal rate of return for NIST's investments is 0.536 or 53.6%.

6.2   Discussion and conclusion

The benefits of roughly $250 billion are substantial, but they are not unusually large. First, observe that those benefits are a cumulative total of annual benefits earning interest at the social rate of return over two decades. To provide perspective, consider that for fiscal year 2017, Microsoft had $90.0 billion in revenue and $22.3 billion in operating income.[7] A company that annually earned operating income of $20 billion in 2017 constant dollars over the two decades from 1998 through 2017 would have $820 billion by 2017 if the annual income were invested and cumulated at 7%.[8]

Second, in many ways the estimated benefit is a very conservative, lower-bound estimate. This is the result both of self-imposed restrictions and limits on required data. Some of the most important limitations were the following:

1. *Self-imposed limit on wider economic extrapolations* — The $250 billion as of 2017 was projected for just those sectors of the economy where there were 10 or more respondents to the survey about the AES benefits.

2. *Partial responses from survey participants* — Many of the respondents, while providing enough information to quantify some of their benefits, also acknowledged other benefits but could not, or in any case did not, provide the information necessary to quantify those benefits. For example, many respondents reported that buyers were willing to pay more for FIPS validated (CA/MVP) cryptographic hardware or software, yet for various reasons could

---

[7] https://www.microsoft.com/investor/reports/ar17/index.html. Accessed May 5, 2018.

[8] Note the analogy with our earlier computation where the present value of an organization's benefits in 2017 is $PVbnft_{2017} = \sum_{t=1998}^{2017} benefit_t \times (1.07)^{2017-t}$.

not provide all of the information needed to convert into quantified benefits their reported estimate of the percentage of the value of their cryptographic products and services that was due to the FIPS validation.

Reasons included the confidentiality of the information in many cases, but also for many products, the cryptographic capabilities are built in and are not priced separately. As a result, respondents would not attempt to provide the information about the annual revenues earned from the cryptographic hardware and/or software modules that they produced.

Further, many of the supply-side respondents (30) provided very complete information about the pricing of their cryptographic modules, but then did not provide detailed information about the number of clients that were paying for the use of those modules. As a consequence, the measured benefits greatly underestimate the supply-side respondents' AES benefits resulting, because their customers value validation testing. The benefits for supply-side respondents because AES stimulated the expansion of their international markets are also greatly underestimated, because of the same incompleteness in the information about the annual revenues that are generated by the respondents' cryptographic hardware and software modules.

3. *Authors use of lower bound or conservative interpretations of survey data* — One major example lies with the data regarding consumers of cryptographic services, and their AES benefits from reduced interoperability costs and from reduced numbers of breaches. Respondents typically held the view that interoperability costs and security breaches increase when their data centers must deal with a greater number of different encryption networks that use different encryption algorithms. Many of the respondents reported that such complexity causes both interoperability costs and breaches to increase exponentially. Some reported that the costs and the breaches would increase linearly with the number of different encryption networks with which their data centers deal. No respondent, however, could quantify the exponent for

the commonly expected exponential increases, so to be very conservative, linear relationships were assumed when estimating the avoided interoperability costs and the avoided breaches.

Further, although many respondents reported that absent AES there would have been many additional strong encryption algorithms in use, the authors conservatively assumed that absent AES there would have been just one additional strong encryption algorithm with which the data centers had to deal.

Evidence supports that estimated AES benefits are clearly underestimates. The survey responses support the conclusion that NIST's investment in AES has been repaid many times over, with economy-wide benefits exceeding NIST's costs by a multiple well in excess of the extrapolated benefit-to-cost ratio of roughly 2,000.[9]

---

[9]Although the conservative lower bound refers directly to the comparison of the benefits to NIST's costs, the overall picture of a large social benefit relative to costs would be essentially unchanged if other social costs, such as the National Security Agency's contribution to the development of AES, were included.

7

Overall Economic Impact Assessment Conclusions

In 1996, members of economic policy establishment are reported to have been in the midst a long-brewing policy crisis that pitted Federal law enforcement and intelligence agencies against commercial encryption hardware and software developers that were unhappy with export controls.[1] That year NIST launched an innovative effort to replace the Federal Government's standard encryption algorithm — DES, FIPS-46-3 — by means of an open international competition. The competition was the first of its kind, through which NIST would ultimately choose an algorithm designed by two Belgian cryptographers. This significantly stronger algorithm would be endorsed by NIST as the Advanced Encryption Standard, FIPS-197, in 2001. The rudiments of cryptography, and the many facets of its role in industry — from both the developers' and users' perspectives — are discussed as background in the preliminary chapters of this monograph.

This monograph evaluates NIST's AES program initiative as though it were a private sector investment decision and provides economic valuations for Net Present Value (NPV), Internal Rate of Return (IRR), and Benefit-to-Cost ratio (B/C). By treating the Federal investment in

---

[1]Levy, op. cit., and Smid, op. cit.

the AES program as though it were a private investment decision, analysis of the survey data collected for this monograph supports the conclusion that NIST's investment of public resources has been successful.

The NPV metric (for our lower-bound economic impact approach (Section 6.1, Table 6.1), based only on the estimates provided by 74 survey respondents), says in effect that if, in 1996, NIST AES program managers could have projected the actual timing and size of the economic benefits (costs avoided) they would have valued the project at $844,500,000, net of costs incurred. To provide perspective about the performance of the AES program, consider 12 other NIST infra-technology projects for which NPV was calculated (1999–2011). For the 12 projects, the median NPV was $48.5M, with NPV's ranging from $3.5M to $773M.[2]

Similarly, another investment decision metric, the IRR, indicates that the return on NIST's AES investment over the period from 1996 to 2017 has been approximately 81%. The IRR is the interest rate (also called the "discount rate") that would reduce the projected NPV of the AES program in 1996 to zero and reduce the B/C ratio to one. Stated differently, it is the discount rate for which the investment would breakeven. In contrast, the hurdle rate for public investment projects is 7%. That hurdle rate is the actual discount rate, also called the social required rate of return, that is used to value public investments and becomes a threshold rate of return for a public investment project. As a guide to making an investment decision on a public or private project, if the IRR is higher than the discount rate, the project is acceptable because the project earns a rate of return greater than its cost of capital. An IRR of 81% is obviously well over the government-mandated threshold of a 7% rate of return. For comparison with the 81% IRR for the AES program, consider 37 NIST infra-technology projects evaluated for IRR over as many years; for those projects, the median IRR was 117%, and the rates ranged from 32% to 1056%.[3]

---

[2]https://www.nist.gov/director/outputs-and-outcomes-nist-laboratory-research, updated by the authors.

[3]Ibid.

Finally, the B/C ratio, 28.6/1 for the AES project lower-bound case, says that for every \$1 dollar of costs expended by NIST's AES program (1996–2017), almost \$29 dollars of social benefits have been returned. For projects with the same costs, those with the highest B/C ratios would be chosen first when there is an investment budget constraint. Of 23 NIST projects evaluated for B/C, the median metric was 11, with the B/C ratios ranging from 3 to 113.[4] Because projects differ in size, the NPV metric discussed above would in practice be the one used for ranking projects, but the comparisons for the IRR and B/C ratios provide useful benchmarks and augment the understanding of the project's performance.

Considering the most conservative basis (using only the 74 respondents that provided information about their benefits from AES) for evaluating NIST's decision to invest public resources in the AES program, over the program's history, those investments have had a relatively high economic impact. On that basis alone, the impacts of NIST's efforts are considerably underestimated. A truer sense of the social returns to the AES program are obtained by, first, extrapolating the benefits for an additional 95 respondents (that provided sufficient information about their activities and organizational type) to have an estimate of the benefits for all 169 (74 + 95) respondents to the economic impact survey, and, second, by extrapolating the benefits for the larger national economy.

Combining the information from the 74 survey respondents used to calculate the NPV, IRR, and B/C metrics just discussed, with the information provided by the additional 95 less complete survey responses, analogous metrics were developed for the combined group of 169 respondents. Developing the metrics for the larger group of respondents required a reconceptualization of the NPV metric. In the brief discussion of NPV above, the authors envisioned the AES program managers as standing in 1996 and looking to the future and knowing what we now know retrospectively (based on survey data) to be the NPV of the AES program, cumulating the appropriately discounted

---

[4]Ibid.

annual information about inflation-adjusted 2017 dollars. That NPV
was $844,500,000.

Extrapolating this result to all 169 survey respondents and then
beyond that to the larger economy requires the following perspective.
Rather than looking from the initiation of the project in 1996 into
to the future, envision NIST managers in 2017 looking back (after
the years of costs and benefits from 1996 through 2017) at the 1996
net economic value of $844,500,000 actually achieved and asking, "If
that amount had been invested and annually earned the cost of capital
required of government technology investments (7%), what would be the
inflation-adjusted value of that investment today in 2017?" Answering
this question gives the impact of the AES program a more contemporary
meaning.

The result of performing that operation on the series of cumulated
benefits extrapolated for the 169 survey respondents finds that present
value of *benefits* from today's perspective is approximately $8.9 billion.
On the other hand, the present value of NIST's *costs* from today's
perspective is $127 million. Thus, the NPV from today's perspective
is $8,772,000,000; the B/C ratio is therefore 70.2/1; and a measure
(explained in detail in Section 6.1) of the IRR for the alternative investment perspective is 31%; all are indicators of a substantial economic
impact.

Extending the approach of looking back from 2017 to the larger
national economy required the selection of economic sectors best represented by the 169 survey respondents. The economic sectors represented
by 10 or more survey respondents include the following: agriculture; construction; manufacturing; retail trade; transportation and warehousing;
information; real estate rental and leasing; professional, scientific, and
technical services; management services; waste management; educational
services; and arts and entertainment. Looking at the present value of
benefits and costs from 2017's perspective for these economic sectors
finds that the present value of *benefits* rises to approximately $251
billion while the present value of NIST's *costs* from today's perspective
remains the same at $127 million. Therefore, the NPV of the benefits of
the AES program to the national economy from today's perspective is
$250,473,200,000; the B/C ratio is roughly 1976/1; and the appropriate,

alternative (explained in Section 6.1) IRR and investing proceeds at the social rate of return is 53.6%.

As substantial as these impact metrics are, they are nevertheless conservative lower bound estimates of actual economic impact for reasons explained in Section 6.2. In brief, in all cases the choice was made to interpret survey responses in the most conservative light. In other words, if the analyst had a choice between a high value and a low value in a response, the low value was selected.

Second, many respondents provided some useful information but not enough to directly quantify the economic benefits they enjoyed. The reasons they did not provide quantifiable impact information are numerous. Respondents' recognition of benefits and yet not being able to quantify them is a problem that has affected economic impact assessments since economists first undertook them.[5] The fact that many respondents did provided information to enable making direct impact assessments illustrates that whatever the reasons for non-responses were, they are not binding on all respondents in roughly similar situations. Survey questions for economic impact assessments tend to require respondents' concentration and at times imagination, and the application of those qualities requires time which is in short supply among busy survey populations.

Finally, even in the case of benefits scaled to the level of the economy, a conservative choice was made to restrict benefits to only those industrial sectors represented by 10 or more survey respondents. For economic sectors with fewer than 10 respondents, we know that these sectors of the economy have benefited from AES too, but we have not extrapolated benefits for them.

The creation of new technology — typically a virtual partnership of public and private fundings, and increasingly a formal partnership[6] — is the single most important contributor to the nation's long-term

---

[5]See, Edwin Mansfield *et al.*, "Social and Private Rates of Return from Industrial Innovations," *The Quarterly Journal of Economics,* Vol. 91, No. 2 (May 1977), pp. 221–240.

[6]U.S. National Science Foundation, Division of Science Resources Studies, *Strategic Research Partnerships: Proceedings from an NSF Workshop,* NSF 01-336.

economic growth path.[7] Spending Federal tax dollars in pursuit of NIST's mission to promote U.S. innovation, industrial competitiveness, and economic security promotes long-term growth. From the most conservative assessment of economic impact presented here to the most carefully extrapolated impacts, NIST's decision in 1996 to structure an internationally competitive search for a sufficiently strong information encryption standard was, and continues to be, an exceptional economic success.

---

[7]Link and Siegel, op. cit.

Appendices

A

Switching Costs and the Transition to AES: The Case of Financial Industry Encryption Standards

Introduction

At the outset of this assessment, the existence of effectively two cryptographic standards (TDES and AES) was perplexing. This case study attempts to come to terms with two encryption standards from an economic perspective.

As discussed at length in Section 2, Background, in the face of fairly dramatic changes in the cryptographic policy environment since the announcement of NIST's first encryption standard (DES) in 1976 — including the commercialization and internationalization of cryptography, the looming digital revolution, and citizens' growing concern (as consumers and business owners) about the problem and costs of compromised confidentiality, integrity, and authenticity — the forces of cryptographic innovation striving to develop stronger encryption, confronted the installed base of DES-based encryption systems.

Hypothetically, NIST could have chosen to wipe the slate clean and require all Federal users to incorporate the AES algorithm into their encryption systems; however, NIST chose to accommodate agencies and suppliers facing high switching costs by slowly and incrementally raising the acceptable key strengths of TDES-based encryption systems.

By effectively choosing both AES and TDES as acceptable symmetric block ciphers, NIST recognized the high switching costs that would be borne by organizations locked-in to DES-based encryption systems, and, for organizations unencumbered by significant switching costs on both the demand and supply sides of the encryption systems market, offered a path to dramatically reduced information security risk along with improved processing performance. The following sections explore the economic logic of that decision as it played out in the financial industry.

The financial industry adopts DES

NIST published DES (FIPS-46) in January 1977, and it became the standard cryptographic algorithm for the financial services industry to protect sensitive customer data. DES was adopted as the ANSI X3.32 Data Encryption Algorithm (DEA) in 1981. The banking and financial industry's standards body, ANSI's ASC X9 (hereafter X9) followed with the development of related standards for message authentication (X9.9-1994), key management (X9.17-1995), and wholesale financial message encryption (X9.23-1995).[1]

Banking automated teller machines (ATM) were largely designed to operate on DES and TDES encryption systems. In the period 1975–1997 the number of ATMs grew from approximately 4,000 to 200,000 nationally.[2] The growth in the number of ATMs reflects the growth of all manner of point-of-sale transactions (debit or credit cards) wherever they occur: gas stations, grocery stores, and restaurants to name a few. The use of bank cards in place of cash was protected by DES and TDES encryption, however as mentioned previously, serious threats arose in the 1990s challenging DES security. In 1997 and again in 1999, the RSA Security Corporation sponsored competitions that produced successful brute force attacks on DES, cracking the cipher in less than 24 hours.[3] The financial industry and the Federal Government understood these

---

[1] *Technical Report: Migration from DES* (TR-37 2009), Accredited Standards Committee X9, Inc.

[2] Leech and Chinworth, op. cit., p. 26.

[3] For the 1997 event a $250,000 computer built by the Electronic Frontier Foundation (EFF) decrypted a DES-encoded message in 56 hours. In 1999 this was improved to 22 hours through a combination of 100,000 networked PCs and the

demonstrations as a harbinger that the DES life cycle (its "crypto-period") was reaching its end. The events instigated X9 to withdraw several DES-based standards. In addition, the Federal Reserve Bank, NIST, and the American Bankers Association issued recommendation letters, recommending migration from DES to Triple DES.[4]

It comes as somewhat of a surprise then to find that industry contacts consistently mention the financial sector, particularly ATM and chip card hardware, as the slowest sector to make the switch to AES. Why? From an economic perspective, the answer in a nutshell is "switching costs." This appears to be the case for the financial industry, and it is suspected to be the case for other sectors where TDES maintained its prevalence. As discussed in Section 5, Survey Findings, many private sector consumers of AES did not switch from TDES until 2010 or later. For the financial sector, the massive network of encrypted hardware and software assets built up over two decades was geared to DES. Like the momentum that requires a big ship to turn slowly in a wide arch, so the time and costs of switching from TDES to AES requires a two-standards solution until 2030. In terms of economic impact, the slow pace of adoption in some sectors pushes the beneficial effects of AES to a later, and thus shorter, period in the assessment timeframe.

Transitioning from DES to TDES to AES

Although TDES is essentially running DES encryption multiple times, a transition from DES to TDES is technically complex, involving changes in the way the algorithm works and in its modes of operation. That complexity could be amplified depending on, for example, the cryptographic schemes for key management employed by user organizations.[5]

EFF machine. Susan Landau, "Standing the Test of Time: The Data Encryption Standard," *Notices of the AMS*, Vol. 47, No.3, March 2000, pp. 341–349.

[4] Accredited Standards Committee X9, op. cit., p. xv.

[5] Ibid. Four modes of operation are discussed in the X9 technical report: Triple DEA Electronic Code Book (TECB), Triple DEA Cipher Block Chaining (TCBC), Triple DEA Cipher Feed Back (TCFB), and Triple DEA Output Feed Back (TOFB). Three key management schemes are also described: Fixed Transaction Key Method, Master Key/Session Key, and Derived Unique Key Per Transaction (DUKPT).

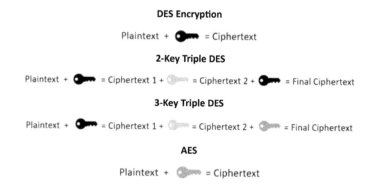

Figure A.1: The "Keys" to high switching costs.

It is helpful to understand how cryptographic keys are employed in DES and TDES and how this contrasts with AES.

Figure A.1 uses colors to illustrate how keys are used in each algorithm; it does not delve into the fundamental differences between DES/TDES and AES encryption rounds and permutations. DES operates with one 56-bit key in a very straightforward manner. Triple DES uses either two or three 56-bit keys and has multiple encryption rounds. 2-Key TDES effectively achieves a 112-bit key strength, while 3-Key TDES holds 168-bit key strength. Finally, AES uses a single 128, 192, or 256-bit key.

Due to its underlying design, not strictly related to key size, AES enables a more secure and efficient encryption process in software implementations.[6] In a simple laptop application, encrypting approximately 1000-byte blocks of plaintext, 3-Key TDES runs approximately three times slower than DES, which is not surprising given, 3-Key TDES runs the DES algorithm three times. AES-128 runs six times faster than 3-Key TDES.[7]

---

[6] According to one assessment, TDES takes three times as much CPU power compared with its DES predecessor. The authors of the assessment regard this as a "significant performance hit." Hamdan O. Alanazi, B. B. Zaidan, A. A. Zaidan, Hamid A. Jalab, M. Shabbir and Y. Al-Nabhani, "New Comparative Study Between DES, 3DES and AES within Nine Factors," *Journal of Computing*, Vol. 2, Issue 3, March 2010, pp. 2151–9617.

[7] Personal communication with Eric Burger, May 8, 2018.

By all accounts, the overall enterprise of converting from DES to TDES was a gargantuan task. A 2009 X9 report worried that, "there are still implementers who have not migrated [from DES]."[8] According to an industry representative, the transition from single DES to TDES involved a "hefty expense" for the industry:

> The key size [effectively] doubled [or tripled], so every application and device involved in the message flow had to be addressed. Hardware where a PIN is entered (ATM or POS) or translated (bank, processor, network, and issuer hardware security module) had to be upgraded and every piece of the software that communicated in or with those devices had to support longer key field in the message and differentiate between the key types. Any database where keys are stored had to support both old and new as well.[9]

An industry observer, reporting in 2008, estimated that the burden on ATM operators of complying with TDES would be thousands to millions of dollars in ATM fleet upgrades, depending on fleet size. In 2005, a large independent ATM supplier estimated that TDES upgrades would take "a few years" and had budgeted $25 million in 2006 for that purpose. In most cases, upgrading machines required new encrypting PIN pads, and software and firmware upgrades to handle effectively longer encryption keys. In 2008 estimates of TDES upgrade costs were between $700 and $2,000 per machine.[10]

Why Was TDES Retained?

First and foremost, TDES has been retained because it provided, and continues to provide, information security. Over time, the 2-Key TDES option was abandoned (disallowed by NIST after December 31, 2010).

---

[8]Ibid., p. 22.

[9]Personal communications with an X9-affiliated financial industry encryption systems expert, April 29–May 2, 2018. (The individual's name is withheld as a condition of several email exchanges.)

[10]Gary Wollenhaupt, "Triple DES: Too High to Comply?," *ATM Marketplace*, July 9, 2008. https://www.atmmarketplace.com/articles/triple-des-too-high-to-comply/.

In 2008, some weaknesses in 3-Key TDES were exposed having to do with the encryption of a large number of blocks of plaintext. That year X9 withdrew its TDES Modes of Operation standard (X9.52-1998) and replaced it with a NIST special publication that recognized and addressed the problem. In 2017 that same special publication was revised and made additional adjustments to the secure threshold for the number of plaintext blocks TDES could be used on.[11] The announcement advised all TDES users to migrate to AES as soon as possible.[12]

From an economic perspective, another important reason for the existence of two encryption standards is the high cost of transitioning to the fundamentally different AES algorithm. A well-informed industry participant suggested that the transition from DES to TDES can serve as a model of the complexities and scale of the problem of transitioning to AES. "The pain of the DES-to-TDES upgrade" provided lessons learned; for example, if the difference between DES and TDES in effective key size caused trouble and expense, the transition from TDES to AES entails two entirely different algorithms, "not a matter of a tweak here and there."[13] So it stands to reason that the switching costs for organizations substantially invested in TDES encrypted systems have been considerable as they proceed to transition to AES.

The issues involved are discussed today under the rubric of "cryptographic agility:"

> Cryptographic agility refers to how easy it is to evolve or replace the hardware, software, or entire information technology (IT) systems being used to implement cryptographic algorithms or protocols (and, in particular, whether the resulting systems remain "interoperable").[14]

---

[11] Elaine Barker and Nicky Mouha, *Recommendation for the Triple Data Encryption Algorithm (TDEA) Block Cipher*, NIST Special Publication 800-67, Revision 2, November 2017.

[12] https://csrc.nist.gov/news/2017/update-to-current-use-and-deprecation-of-tdea.

[13] Personal communication with X9 expert, op. cit.

[14] *Cryptographic Agility and Interoperability: Proceedings of a Workshop Forum on Cyber Resilience Workshop Series*, Washington, DC: The National Academies Press, 2017, p. 2.

A participant in a recent workshop on cryptographic agility, sponsored by the National Academies of Sciences, Engineering, and Medicine, opined that,

> [R]eplacing a system completely takes a long time because it requires an enormous amount of work... completely replacing a widely deployed system would take at least three years, assuming that there is already a well-tested replacement system ready for deployment, and ten years or more if a new cryptographic approach had to be developed from scratch starting at the time of the discovery of the vulnerability in the old system.[15]

Given the continued security strength of 3-Key TDES, and at the risk of projecting a current understanding onto those anticipating TDES and its eventual replacement by AES in the late 1990s, the perception that transitioning to a new standard "from scratch" was very expensive and could take 10 years to develop and deploy would seem to explain why X9 and much of the financial industry stayed the course with TDES, even in the face of a demonstrably vulnerable DES, and with the AES competition underway. History demonstrates that developing the AES standard took significantly less than 10 years, only four years "from scratch," and moreover, that deploying products with AES was achievable within months for prepared organizations. Hence, there have been two symmetric block cipher encryption standards since 2001.

---

[15]Ibid., p. 8. These views were expressed by Bob Blakley, CitiGroup, Inc., presumably representing views held by other members of the financial services community.

B

Economic Impact Metrics

The economic impact metrics in this monograph are calculated from a time series of costs and benefits in constant dollars. They represent "real" rates of return. In contrast, "nominal" rates of return would be based on time series of current dollars (the dollars of the year in which the benefits were realized or in which the costs were incurred).

Internal rate of return (IRR)

The IRR is the value of the discount rate, i, that equates the net present value (NPV) of a stream of all net benefits associated with an investment project to zero. The time series runs from the beginning of the project, $t = 0$, to a milestone terminal point, $t = n$. Net benefits refer to total benefits (B) less total costs (C) in each time period. Mathematically,

$$\text{NPV} = [(B_0 - C_0)/(1+i)^0] + \cdots + [(B_n - C_n)/(1+i)^n] = 0 \quad \text{(B.1)}$$

where $(B_t - C_t)$ represents the net benefits associated with the project in year t, and n represents the number of time periods (years in most cases) being considered in the evaluation.

For unique solutions of i, from Equation (B.1), the IRR can be compared to a value, r, that represents the opportunity cost of funds

invested by the technology-based public institution. Thus, if the opportunity cost of funds is less than the social rate of return, the project
was worthwhile from an ex post social perspective.

Benefit-to-cost ratio (B/C)

The ratio of benefits-to-costs is precisely that, the ratio of the present
value of all measured benefits to the present value of all costs. Both
benefits and costs are referenced to the initial time period, $t = 0$, as:

$$B/C = \left[\Sigma_{t=0 \text{ to } t=n} B_t/(1+r)^t\right] / \left[\Sigma_{t=0 \text{ to } t=n} C_t/(1+r)^t\right]. \quad (B.2)$$

A benefit-to-cost ratio of 1 implies a break-even project. Any project with
$B/C > 1$ is a relatively successful project. Fundamental to implementing
the ratio of benefits-to-costs is a value for the discount rate, r.

While the discount rate representing the opportunity cost for public
funds could differ across a portfolio of public investments, the calculated
metrics in this monograph follow the guidelines set forth by the Office
of Management and Budget: Constant-dollar benefit–cost analyses of
proposed investments and regulations should report net present value
and other outcomes determined using a real discount rate of 7%.[1]

Net present value (NPV)

The information developed to determine the benefit-to-cost ratio can
be used to determine net present value as:

$$\text{NPV} = B - C. \quad (B.3)$$

---

[1] Office of Management and Budget (OMB), Circular No. A-94 Revised,
"Guidelines and Discount Rates for Benefit-Cost Analysis of Federal Programs,"
October 29, 1992.

C

Understanding the Alternative IRR

The alternative IRR is a constrained and dampened IRR. As compared with the traditional internal rate of return, the alternative rate of return is much lower because it constrains all of the benefits to be reinvested, at the time they are realized, at the relatively low social required rate of return, and then the alternative internal rate of return is for the rate of growth in the returns over the entire period from 1996 to 2017, with the growth constrained to the lower 7% rate of return from the realization of the benefits until 2017.

Rather than "take down" the benefits in the year received, annual benefits must be invested at the social rate of return and allowed to grow until 2017. The benefits are cumulated in that way and then they are "taken down" in 2017. Thus, with a project such as the AES project, an initial investment pays a very large return in a few years. The traditional internal rate of return reflects that high rate of return when relatively few dollars invested initially yield a great many dollars in a few years. However, with the alternative internal rate of return, those great many dollars are not taken down or withdrawn at the time of the benefit and the high rate of return then observed. Instead, they are reinvested at the relatively low social required rate of return (the long-term average private rate of return on investment in the U.S. economy).[1] Then, years later in 2017, the return is taken down, i.e., withdrawn, and after years of growing at the lower rate of return the overall annual rate of return is dampened from what it would have been if the return had been withdrawn when it originally occurred and the internal rate of return recorded at that time.

The alternative internal rate of return is the rate at which the discounted present value of costs at time zero — the beginning of the investments in 1996 — would have had to grow to release the cumulated value of the annual benefits that are taken down in 2017. In contrast, the traditional metric assumes that the benefits are growing at a certain rate — that they can be reinvested at that rate throughout the investment period until 2017 — making the entire stream of benefits with its returns dispersed over the years from the initiation of the project until 2017, have a present value in 1996 equal to the present value of the stream of costs at that time. In the alternative, the annual benefits must be reinvested at the 7% annual rate of return and allowed to cumulate until 2017. Then, at that time, with the growth rate in returns dampened to the 7% annual return from their actual occurrence until 2017, we find the rate that would make the cumulated 2017 amount's present value in 1996 equal to the present value of the stream of costs in 1996.

Here is a simple example. Imagine for $100 invested now, there is a benefit of $150 in one year and then a benefit of $225 in two years. The conventional internal rate of return is r such that $100 = 150/(1+r)+225/(1+r)^2$. Then $r = 1.42705$ or 142.7%. The alternative internal rate of return is r such that $100 = ((150)*(1.07)+225)/(1+r)^2$. Then $r = 0.963415$ or 96.3%. Even in this simple example, there is a dramatic dampening effect by not taking down the benefit of $150 in a year and reckoning the rate of return, but instead reinvesting it at the lower 7% per annum rate of return and then finding the rate of return over the longer period during which the return was constrained to the low 7% per annum.

---

[1]Link and Scott, 2011, op. cit.

D

Two-Stage Procedure for Extrapolating the Economic Benefits of NIST's AES Program

Methodological rationale for benefits extrapolation

The benefit estimates for the 169 survey respondents are understood as random variables subject to a great deal of uncertainty. The most important part of that uncertainty cannot be quantified because it is the uncertainty associated with the original set of 74 respondents that provided sufficient information to estimate AES benefits. Each of those 74 respondents typically did not provide enough information to quantify all of the types of benefits addressed in the survey. Although they often acknowledged that the benefits existed, they did not attempt to answer the survey questions that would have allowed a quantitative estimate. Even when sufficient information was provided to form an estimate of a particular type of benefit, the respondents were providing their knowledgeable assessment of the information, and those assessments are subject to uncertainty.

For the additional 95 respondents that provided the information used in the estimated model of benefits, the 95 predicted values for the present value of benefits in 2017 which are random variables, and there are two sources of their variance. One source of variance in the predicted values is the uncertainty associated with the estimated coefficients in our estimated model. The other source of variance is the residual error, the error in the estimated equation of our ordinary least squares model. Thus, the total for the estimated benefits for the two groups of respondents — the 74 respondents (for which we had their reported benefits) and the 95 respondents (who did not provide information about their benefits but did provide the information needed for the variables in our estimated model) is a random variable. It will have variance due to the incompleteness and uncertainty in the survey responses from the original 74 respondents, and then additionally from the two sources of variance in the 95 estimated benefits using our model.

The economic impact metrics reported in the body of this monograph should be considered to underestimate the AES benefit in the sense that typically respondents recognized, but could not quantify, many of the benefits asked about in the survey. Also, the impact metrics are subject to great uncertainty. They are the expected value of a portion of the benefits, and the probability distribution for that portion of the benefits assigns probability to much lower as well as much higher ranges for the benefits, although we cannot sensibly quantify the uncertainty because the most important part of it comes from the uncertainty surrounding the survey responses of the original 74 respondents rather than from the estimation of a formal model.

First-stage extrapolation procedure for 169 survey respondents

To estimate the benefits for the 95 survey respondents that did not provide information from which cost avoidance benefits could be directly estimated, the first step was to take the time series of annual benefits (in 2017 constant dollars) for each of our 74 respondents that provided data from which benefits estimates could be derived directly, and convert it to the present value of those benefits in 2017 (referred to in the body of this monograph as "cumulative benefits"). That present value of benefits in 2017 for each of the 74 observations is the value that would be generated by 2017 if each respondent's annual benefits, in its stream of benefits from 1998 to 2017, were invested at the real social annual rate of return of 7% and allowed to grow until 2017.[1]

The second step was to use those 74 respondents' cumulative benefits and industry sectors and respondent types to estimate a model of the 2017 present value of benefits. The model is an ordinary least squares regression of the 2017 present value of respondents' benefits as a function of the type of respondent (private consumer, private producer/developer, private integrator, public consumer, academic or independent cryptographer, and cryptographic testing consultants), and the industrial classification category(ies) for the respondent. The estimated model is significant at the classical level of significance (against the null hypothesis of no effect for the model's variables, the probability of a greater F-statistic is $0.003 < 0.01$).[2]

The third step was to use the estimated model to predict the benefits for the 95 respondents that did not provide enough information to construct any of the benefits shown in Table 5.3 in the body of this monograph but did provide the information for the variables used in the estimated model of benefits. Namely, for these additional 95 observations, the type of respondent (private consumer, private producer/developer, private integrator, public consumer, academic or independent cryptographer, and cryptographic testing consultant) and

---

[1]Thus, the present value of an organization's benefits in 2017 is $PVbnft_{2017} = \sum_{t=1998}^{2017} benefit_t \times (1.07)^{2017-t}$.

[2]The model uses ordinary least squares to estimate, as a function of the sector or sectors of the economy and the type of respondent, the present value in 2017 of a respondent's cumulated benefits over the years: $PVbnft_{2017} = f$ (sector effects, respondent type effects) with the public administration sector effect (NAICS sector 92) and the public agency respondent effect left in the intercept and with fitted effects for the remaining sectors (NAICS sectors Construction, 23; Manufacturing, 31–33; Retail trade, 44–45; Information, 51; Finance and insurance, 52; Professional, scientific, and technical services, 54; Educational services, 61; Health care and social assistance, 62; and Arts, entertainment, and recreation, 71) for which we have observations among the 74 respondents, and for the remaining respondent types (private consumers, private producer/developer, private integrator, and the combined academic/consultant categories). Not unexpectedly given the relatively small number of observations and relatively large number of effects fitted, many of the individual effects estimated are not significant statistically, but the F-statistic for their collective significance is statistically significant: $n = 74$, $F(13, 60) = 2.83$, probability of a greater F statistic $= 0.0031$, $R^2 = 0.38$.

its industrial classification were reported. The predicted benefits for these additional 95 respondents are added to the benefits for the 74 respondents to produce an estimate of the benefits for 169 observations.

Second-stage extrapolation procedure for estimating sector-wide economic benefits of 169 survey respondents

The extrapolation of benefits to whole sectors of the economy began with a data set for all 169 $(74 + 95)$ survey respondents where their industrial classifications and their types were known. Added to that data set was the number of employees for each respondent's organization if it was reported. For any respondents that did not report the number of employees, it was estimated with the average of the reported employment for respondents of the same type. More elaborate estimates are precluded by the paucity of the data for the set of 95 respondents.

The 169 respondents are distributed across the broad sectors of the economy as shown in Table 5.4, column 1. Extrapolations of benefits to the sector or broad industry level are developed where 10 or more respondents have activity in that category, in order to make the projections to the sector level based on coverage of a more substantial amount of a sector's economic activity. Thus, an extrapolation of benefits for the following sectors is provided, with the number, n, of respondents used to make the extrapolation shown in parentheses: Manufacturing $(n = 45)$, Information $(n = 47)$, Finance and insurance $(n = 42)$, Professional, scientific, and technical services $(n = 41)$, Educational services $(n = 12)$, Health care and social assistance $(n = 13)$, and Public administration $(n = 16)$.

Many respondents have activity in more than one sector of the economy. For each respondent, a variable z was calculated that equals the number of different sectors in which the respondent operated. Each respondent's cumulative benefits ($PVbnft2017$— the cumulated value at the social rate of return of its annual benefits over the years) was divided by z to have for each of the n respondents, the portion of their benefits to be assigned to each of the sectors where they operate. Note also that within different parts of a sector — the manufacturing sector is a notable example — some respondents are consumers of cryptographic products and services, and some respondents are producers of the products and services.

Table 5.4 shows the extrapolation of AES benefits to sectors of the economy where there are 10 or more respondents with estimated benefits.

Acknowledgements

We are pleased to acknowledge the contributions of Dr. Eric Burger, of Georgetown University's Security and Software Engineering Research Center (S2ERC), for his technical advice and for helping to infuse economically meaningful concepts with equally meaningful technical content during the survey design phase of our research.

Historical background information was provided by public and private sector individuals, who helped anchor our understanding of what was at stake in the decisions to launch the AES initiative, to participate in it, and to adopt AES-based encryption systems. Among current and former NIST personnel, we acknowledge the contributions of Larry Bassham, Lily Chen, Donna Dodson, James Foti, Edward Roback, Matthew Scholl, and Miles Smid. We would like to thank Vincent Rijmen at the University of Leuven, Belgium, one of the co-creators of the winning algorithm for AES, for his insights on AES, the competition, and the cryptographic environment of the 1990s. The following individuals provided insights from the private sector perspective: David Balenson (SRI International), John Callas (Apple), John Green (Hewlett Packard), Marc Ireland (UL Transaction Security), Brian LaMacchia (Microsoft), Lisa Yin (RC6 developer, formerly of RSA Labs), Matt Keller (Corsec), Matthew McGhee (COACT, Inc.), Ari Singer (TrustiPhi), Paul Spaven (3e Technologies International, Inc.), Ashit Vora (Acumen Security), Steven Weingart (Hewlett Packard), and others who wished to remain anonymous. Special thanks to Matt Keller who went the extra mile in providing a sounding board for numerous technology and industry issues as they arose over the course of our research.

We also thank the following individuals and their organizations for their support during the survey phase of our research: Chris Cook (College of Healthcare Information Management Executives, CHIME), Patrick Gaul (National Technology Security Coalition, NTSC), Marie Gilbert (Information Systems Audit and Control Association, ISACA), Matt Keller (Cryptographic Module User Forum, CMUF, and Common Criteria User Forum, CCUF), Alex Morris (Internet Engineering Task Force, IETF), Paul Nikolich (Institute of Electrical and Electronics Engineers, IEEE), Josh Poster (National Council of ISACs, NCI), Douglas Robinson (National Association of State Chief Information Officers, NASCIO), Eileen Sciarra (Information Systems Security Association, ISSA), Foy Shiver (Anti-Phishing Working Group, APWG), Steve Stevens (Accredited Standards Committee X9), and Lynn Terwoerds (Executive Women's Forum on Information Security, EWF).

Finally, Michael Walsh and Kathleen McTigue of NIST's Technology Partnership Office (TPO) offered many helpful suggestions on earlier drafts of this monograph.

Author Biographies

David P. Leech is an independent consultant specializing in discovering the economic impacts of Federal science and technology programs and the targeted assessment of defense-related industries. He has been the principle investigator and project manager for a number of economic impact assessments for the National Institute of Standards and Technology (NIST) and the Air Force Research Laboratory (AFRL). He has conducted numerous industry assessments for the Office of the Secretary of Defense and the Manufacturing Technology Division of AFRL. He has a BA in Economics from the University of Maryland, Baltimore County (UMBC), was a graduate student of political economy at American University and Durham University, and will receive an MA in Humanities from Towson University (2019).

Stacey Ferris is a Certified Public Accountant and Certified Fraud Examiner with primary experience in forensic and business analysis, data analysis, financial and compliance audit, fraud investigation, and management consulting. She received her Masters of Accountancy from Georgia Southern University and a BBA in Accountancy with a minor in Mandarin Chinese from the University of North Georgia. She is a member of the Association of Government Accountant's Blockchain Working Group and her article on blockchain in government was published in the winter 2019 volume of the Journal of Government Financial Managers. This is her premiere contribution to a economic impact study supported by the National Institute of Standards and Technology.

John T. Scott is Professor of Economics, Emeritus, at Dartmouth College, where he joined the faculty in 1977. His teaching and research are in the areas of industrial organization and the economics of technological change. He received the Ph.D. in Economics from Harvard University and the A.B. in Economics and English from the University of North Carolina at Chapel Hill. While a Teaching Fellow at Harvard University, he received the Allyn Young Teaching Prize. He served as the President of the Industrial Organization Society and as an Associate Editor and a member of the editorial boards of the International Journal of Industrial Organization, the Review of Industrial Organization, and The Journal of Industrial Economics. His research has been supported by the National Institute of Standards and Technology, the National Science Foundation, the National Research Council of the National Academies, the World Bank, the United Nations Development Programme, and the Organization for Economic Co-operation and Development. He served as an economist at the Board of Governors of the Federal Reserve System and at the Federal Trade Commission.